AF265201

BIOGRAPHICAL

)25     --Born, Prescott, Ontario
)51     --B.A., University of Western Ontario
)52     --M.A., University of Western Ontario
)53-55 --School of Graduate Studies, University of Toronto
    56
)55-56 --Lecturer, Department of Philosophy, University of Toronto.

THESIS

<u>Space and Time in the Philosophies of Kant and Bergson</u>

(Abstract)


This thesis undertakes a systematic investigation of the theories of space
id time of Kant and Bergson. Its purpose is to exhibit the relation between these
ieories and to show that Bergson's theory may be regarded as a logical develop-
ient of Kant's.

As an essential preliminary to the investigation, an extended discussion of
irtain problems concerning space and time is presented. Of central importance
; the question of whether it is necessary to make a fundamental metaphysical dis-
nction between space and time. It is concluded that the evidence seems to suggest
iat a theory which distinguishes between space and time is more tenable than one
hich treats space and time as exactly analogous elements in a four-dimensional
pace-time manifold. In addition, the preliminary discussion deals with problems
reated by the distinction between space and time. Since Kant and Bergson distin-
iish time from space by recognizing the intrinsic uniqueness of the passage of time,
oth philosophers are faced with the problems resulting from this distinction.

The introductory discussion provides a framework in which the views of
ant and Bergson are examined. First, by vindicating the distinction between space
nd time, it indicates the line which a development of Kant's views may justifiably
ike. Secondly, it uncovers the nature of those difficulties which lead Bergson to
development of Kant's views. Thirdly, it investigates the relationship between
pace and time and the principle of individuation in a manner which provides two
lternative possibilities for the interpretation of Kant's theory of space and time.

It is suggested that a theory of space and time may take two alternative
ositions with respect to the relationship between space and time and the principle
f individuation and other related principles which are the foundation of unity in na-
ire. A theory may take the position that there is a principle of individuation for
pace which accounts for events in time, or that there is a principle of individuation
ir time which accounts for objects in space. In this thesis, the former alternative
; called "possibility A", the latter, "possibility B".

At this point, Kant's views are introduced, and it is argued that his theory
f space and time approximates to possibility B, rather than possibility A. Kant's
ianner of distinguishing between space and time, and his doctrine of inner and outer
ense are examined. It is shown that he conceived of space and time as homogeneous
iedia, and that the distinction between them rests on the point that time has the
iaracteristic of passage, and is uniquely associated with inner experience, while
pace is not. Space and outer sense seem to be, for Kant, an abstract aspect of
iner sense, the peculiar form of which is time.

It is pointed out that Kant's exclusion of space from the account of the schematism of the categories is consistent with possibility B, rather than possibility A. In addition, it is argued that Kant's Copernican revolution and his justification of synthetic _a priori_ knowledge are only possible if he follows possibility B. For Kant must show that _future_ experience will be determined in general in accordance with the categories, and this is only possible if the categories, as rules of synthesis which make for the unity of nature, apply to time rather than space. Otherwise the passage of time might bring about experience not determined in accordance with the categories. In addition Kant's answer to Hume's scepticism, by the same token would not be possible except according to a theory which accepted possibility B. Kant's relevant statements are examined, and the weight of evidence seems to suggest that his theory of space and time approximates to possibility B.

Bergson's views are then introduced, and the striking similarity between Kant and Bergson in closely associating time and inner experience is pointed out. It is shown that Bergson follows Kant closely in holding that the unique character of time is revealed in inner experience which is in time alone. Kant's views on the impossibility of a science of psychology reveal that, for him, inner experience is quite unlike outer experience. Inner experience constitutes an area of appearances, which, although indubitable, are not subject to categorical determination, and hence do not represent possible experience in Kant's sense. Kant and Bergson are in agreement that knowledge appropriate to spatially related objects is inapplicable to the flow of inner experience.

This raises several problems which Kant does not attempt to solve, but which Bergson deals with at length. Kant's Copernican revolution requires that the categories, which arise independently in the nature of human thinking, should apply directly to time itself. Kant's doctrine of the Transcendental Imagination and the Schematism represents an attempt to mediate between the categories with their independent source and the concrete flow of time. But how such mediation is possible remains obscure. Bergson meets this problem by declaring it to be insoluble, a pseudo-problem stemming from a basic misconception of the nature of time.

Kant held that time was adequately representable in terms of concepts appropriate to space. But he was unable to render this doctrine consistent with his view that time is a unique form of sensibility. Bergson's development of Kant's theory consists in large part of showing that the time of inner experience cannot possibly be understood in terms of concepts appropriate to outer sense. Kant had refused to answer the question of how human experience, which is characterized by two different modes of sensibility, namely, inner and outer sense, comes to have a unity. He gives no clear account of the unifying relation between inner and outer sense, and consequently no answer to the question of the relation between time as a unique form of the perpetual flux of inner experience, and the homogeneous time of outer sense. Bergson attempts to answer this question by showing that homogeneous time is a spurious, spatialized concept and by an appeal to intuition. Spatial concepts falsify time, but the relationship between space and outer sense, and time and inner sense may be grasped by a metaphysical intuition which reveals how the concrete flow of time is broken up into discrete spatial parts. Bergson, as well as Kant, subscribes to possibility B, in holding that the intellect applies to the basic flow of time. But for Bergson, this application constitutes a falsification of the metaphysical reality of time.

Bergson's view that time is ultimate reality represents a consistent development of Kant's theory of space and time. For Bergson's theory of time as a con-

crete process of change, which is glimpsed in inner experience, takes advantage of
the fact that, for Kant, the appearances and changes of inner experience are beyond
the pale of cognition  Inner experience, for Kant, has a status exactly analogous to
the status of things-in-themselves in being incapable of being known by means of the
categories  Yet inner experience is indubitably real since it is actually experienced
as a continuous flux, a point which Kant often stresses  Bergson's theory carries
to its logical conclusion the point that beyond the sphere of conceptual determination,
there can be no distinction between form and content  Thus time is not merely the
real _form_ of inner sense, as it is for Kant, but is concrete change itself as revealed
in the indivisible succession of conscious states  Time is real  in itself  because it
is implied in consciousness itself

Bergson's close association of consciousness with the flow of time is related
to another aspect of Kant's thought  Kant distinguishes between inner sense and apperception, but fails to stress that inner sense is <u>conscious</u> inner sense  Bergson
seizes upon this point, combining it with Kant's view that inner sense reveals a perpetual flux which is not cognizable  Kant's distinction between inner sense and apperception, thus represents the seed of Bergson's radical separation of the intellect
and real time revealed in inner consciousness

Bergson erects the apprehension of the change revealed in inner experience
into a supreme metaphysical principle  He thus follows Kant's view that a metaphysics which would penetrate beyond appearance to reality itself must be intuitive  But
whereas Kant thought this intuition would have to be an intellectual intuition, Bergson,
stressing the consciousness of change in inner experience, argues that the intuition
is non-intellectual  He rejects Kant's doctrine of judgment, and a logic of temporal
process, holding that intellectual thinking is through-and-through a spatialization of
a fundamentally non-spatial reality  Following this line of thought Bergson tries to
show how matter and the intellect itself arise from the basic flow of <u>duration</u> (la
durée)  He thus denies the independent origin of the pure concepts of the understanding, and tries to show that logic itself is derivative rather than fundamental  Bergson's development of some aspects of Kant's thought thus ends in a view which would
have been anathema to Kant

GRADUATE STUDIES

<u>Major Subject</u>
      Systematic Philosophy and Metaphysics   Professor F  H  Anderson
                                                   Professor T  A  Goudge

<u>Minor Subjects</u>
      M  A , University of Western Ontario (Subject of thesis   Process in the
      philosophies of Hegel and Whitehead)

      English Language and Literature       Professor A  S  P  Woodhouse,
                                            Professor F  E  L  Priestley

SPACE AND TIME

IN

THE PHILOSOPHIES OF KANT AND BERGSON


BY

Clifford Wellington Webb


A thesis submitted in conformity
with the requirements for the degree of

Doctor of Philosophy

in the

University of Toronto

1956

# C O N T E N T S


CHAPTER ONE:     INTRODUCTION


CHAPTER TWO:     PRELIMINARY DISCUSSION OF THE DISTINCTION

                 BETWEEN SPACE AND TIME

    1.  General Features of the Distinction between
        Space and Time

    2.  Similarities and Differences between Space
        and Time

    3.  The Direction of Time and the Problem of
        Individuation


CHAPTER THREE:   KANT'S THEORY OF SPACE AND TIME

    1.  Kant's Distinction between Space and Time

    2.  Inner and Outer Sense

    3.  Time and the Unity of Nature


CHAPTER FOUR:    BERGSON'S THEORY OF SPACE AND TIME AND ITS

                 RELATION TO THAT OF KANT

    1.  Time and Inner Experience

    2.  The Cognitive Representation of Time

    3.  Primordial Time and the Spatializing Intellect


NOTES


BIBLIOGRAPHY

CHAPTER ONE

INTRODUCTIO.

This thesis aims at a systematic investigation of
the theories of space and time of Kant and Bergson.  Its
purpose is to exhibit the relation between these theories,
and to show that Bergson's views may be re_arded as a
logical development of those of Kant.  It should be added
that this endeavour proceeds from a metaphysical standpoint.
The <u>Critique of Pure Reason</u>, regarded as embodying Kant's
mature philosophy, is not looked upon as solely an epistemological treatise.  That this work is concerned with basic
epistemological questions, of course, goes without saying.
That it does not also involve metaphysical principles and
commitments, is here denied.  Thus, for exam le, we take
the view with Gottfried Martin that,

> The question that Kant is asking is not how
> we can know space and time, but quite simply what
> space and time are.  This question has an ontological
> sense. . . 1

Kant's own words, indeed, support this view, for
in the Transcendental Aesthetic he asks, not "hat knowledge do we have of space and time?", but ".hat, then, are
space and time?".  It becomes apparent that Kant does not
merely tell us how space and time figure in human knowledge,
but gives us a view of the natures of space and time,

1

themselves.  It is necessary to emphasize this because various theories of space and time may be presented in different domains of knowledge.  The question of what space and time are is answered differently, for example, in physi and psychology.  Kant offers an answer to this question, however, not merely in the context of some particular subject matter, but in a wider, metaphysical sense.

For this reason, we consider it essential to approa our subject by way of an extended preliminary discussion. In this discussion we shall deal, first, with the general features of the distinction between space and time (Ch.II, Sec. 1); secondly, with the question of their ultimate similarities and differences  (Ch. II, Sec. 2); and thirdly, with certain relations between space, time and change (Ch. Sec. 3).

In connection with the first of these topics, an indication of the chief desiderata of a metaphysical explanation of the distinction between space and time is intended.  One of the central points to be made in this thesis is that Kant's theory of space and time leaves certain problems unsolved.  That is, Kant's explanation does not deal with, indeed, does not even attempt to deal with some of the questions that arise in connection with space and time.  Yet Kant gives us a metaphysical theory of space and time, and a metaphysical account of their distinction.

His views do not pertain merely to space and time as they are dealt with either in physics or psychology. His doctrine is, nevertheless, incomplete as a metaphysical theory . Kant explicitly recognizes that he leaves some questions un-answered. Our preliminary discussion of the general features of the distinction between space and time attempts to clari-fy the nature of these questions.

Bergson's views are here regarded as a development of those of Kant in the sense that Bergson, while agreeing with Kant on fundamental points, goes on to develop a theory which attempts to deal with the questions which Kant left unanswered. Thus Bergson's views differ radically in some respects from those of Kant. Kant's theory of space and time is necessarily limited by the critical position which he adopted. Bergson continues on, beyond the point where Kant stopped, to make statements of a kind which Kant, on principle, would refuse to make. Accepting the premise that unanswered metaphysical questions concerning the re-lationship between space and time require answers, Berg-son's doctrines may be regarded in this respect as a logical development of Kant's. One point, however, needs to be made clear in this connection. This thesis is not specifically an attempt to evaluate the merits of Bergson's development of Kant's views. No defence of either Kant or Bergson is attempted. It is hoped, however, that presentation of the

issues involved in the relation between the theories of these two philosophers will aid the reader in drawing his own conclusions.

With respect to the second set of topics which we consider an essential preliminary to our subject, namely, those concerning the similarities and differences between space and time, it is intended to present some of the important considerations which bear on the question of whether or not a fundamental distinction must be made between space and time.  By a fundamental distinction between space and time, we mean a metaphysical distinction which recognizes that time is intrinsically different from space <u>at</u> <u>least</u> in that it has the characteristic of passage.  It should be added that when it is said that time has the characteristic of passage, it is not meant that time itself changes or passes, which is a rather loose way of expressing a difficult point.  The question of a fundamental distinction between space and time, the crux of which turns on the problem of the passage of time, is discussed quite generally, without specific reference to the two philosophers under examination in this thesis.  Nevertheless, the conclusions derived from this discussion have an important bearing on the main conclusions of the thesis.  Since both Kant and Bergson do make such a fundamental distinction between space and time, the validity of their doing so is an essential

point in judging in what direction a development of Kant's views may justifiably be made. If Kant was wrong in making this distinction, a reconstruction of his philosophy would involve a rejection of the distinction. If Kant was right, however, the only fruitful line of development would be toward a theory which likewise made a fundamental distinction between space and time.

Recent philosophical literature has included notable attempts to show that the analogies between space and time, which will be discussed herein, are not merely superficial, but may be pressed much further beyond the point where they were heretofore thought to break down. It is argued by certain writers that differences which have traditionally been supposed to obtain between space and time, do not, in fact, hold, and that the supposition that there are such differences is the result of insufficient analysis. In connection with this, there is an attempt to show that one characteristic in particular which was formerly thought to mark a fundamental difference between space and time, viz., the characteristic of the passage of time, as opposed to the static quality of space, is not a characteristic of time at all, and does not constitute ground for a differentiation of space and time. In conjunction with this view there has been presented what is termed the "manifold theory". This theory not only denies that time is fundamentally different

from space in that it has the characteristic of passage, but confesses to bafflement as to what a distinction on this ground might mean. The denial of passage is logically associated with the metaphysical theory of a four-dimensional manifold of space-time and is the main point at issue in the problem of whether there is a fundamental distinction between space and time. Upholders of the manifold theory agree that their theory is adequate to account for some distinction between space and time, but they are vague as to what the distinction is. Hence it is difficult to decide whether they have some other metaphysical distinction in mind or not, and still more difficult to imagine what the nature of this other distinction might be.

Arguments advanced in favour of the manifold theory are herein examined with a view to determining their validity. It is maintained that this position has not been demonstrated to be true, and that there are good reasons for rejecting it in favour of the view that there is a fundamental distinction between space and time. It is important to emphasize this because it has been supposed that with some reconstruction Kant's philosophy could be made to accomodate a theory of space-time. In one sense, of course, this is a reasonable supposition. The physical theory of space-time may be accepted without rejecting a fundamental distinction between space and time. As to the further consideration of

whether Kant's epistemology excludes the possibility of non-Euclidean geometries, which a number of scholars have ably dealt with,[3] this issue is other than the one we are considering. We must carefully distinguish the question of whether a theory of space-time, such as has been found useful in physical science, is compatible with Kantian epistemology, from the question of whether a metaphysical theory of space-time, which denies passage, is compatible with Kant's metaphysics of space and time. What we are considering is the possibility of a development of Kant's views which espouses a theory of space-time which utterly obliterates Kant's way of distinguishing between space and time. Such a theory, incorporating some of Kant's critical principles could, no doubt, be formulated. Whether it would be Kantian in the sense of including Kant's metaphysical presuppositions concerning space and time, however, is another question. It is argued herein that a view which fails to make a fundamental distinction between space and time, will, in important respects, be un-Kantian, a departure from Kant rather than a development from him.

It is important to distinguish this issue concerning the passage of time from problems relating to space and time as they are dealt with in physics. Criticism of the philosophical conception of space-time is not necessarily a criticism of the physicists' conception of space-time. The

"manifold theory" which is here discussed is not identical
with the physicists' conception of space-ti.e, although there
are similarities between the two.  For exa.ple, both theories
concur in treating time mathematically as a fourth dimension.
But whereas the physicist's treatment of space and time is
fashioned in conformity with the end of achievin~ the greatest
theoretical generalizations concerning physical events, the
philosopher's conception knows no such limitations.  Thus,
the latter speaks not merely of physical events in space-
time, but of _all_ events as being in space-time.

> I believe that the universe consists, without
> residue, of the spread of events in space-time, and
> that if we thus accept realistically the four-dimensional
> fabric of juxtaposed actualities we can dispense with
> all those dim non-factual categorics which have so be-
> devilled our race: the potential, the subsistential,
> and the influential, the noumenal, the numinous, and
> the non-natural.  4

The metaphysical position which denies the intrinsic uniqueness of time, and represents the universe in the above manner,
is, we shall suggest, without foundation.

But the fundamental distinction between space and
time is likewise important for our purposes in that Bergson's
position leans heavily on it.  It is not too much to say
that the core of Ber son's philosophy lies in his interpretation of time.  Bergson states that he follows Kant's doctrines concerning space, but disagrees with Kant concerning
time.  Nevertheless, they agree that there is a basic difference between the two, and they agree on certain important

features of this distinction, notably, on points concerning
that aspect of time, the characteristic of passage, which
distinguishes it radically from space. Bergson's develop-
ent of the position held by Kant is a development of what
is implicit in a position explicitly and rigorously adopted
by Kant, namely, that there is a fundamental distinction
between space and time. Bergson probes deeper into the nature of this distinction. He sharpens the kind of distinction made by Kant, and argues that if time is something quite
unlike space, it is not even conceivable in terms of space.
This is the point where Kant stopped. With some hesitation,
Kant declares that time is legitimately represented in spatial
terms. But how this is possible in view of the basic kind
of distinction which Kant makes between space and time, remains unexplained. Kant's association of time with inner
sense is at the core of the difficulty, and is, in addition,
one of a number of rather striking similarities between Kant
and Bergson.

That the philosophies of Kant and Bergson have remarkable similarities is a point made by A. D. Lindsay. He
also points out the other element in Bergson's thought
which allows the doctrines of the two philosophers to be
considered systematically in a relationship of development,
namely, Bergson's critical attitude.

not without suggesting any comparison in importance between Kant and Bergson, there is this resemblance
between the , that much of the interest of Bergson's
work consists in his statement and exposition of antinomies to be found in present-day philosophy, that
as the best road to the solution of these antinomies
he offers a new statement of the task or problem of
philosophy, and propounds a new method.  Like Kant,
his work professes to be critical: to find the main
source of difficulties in an uncriticized assumption. 5

Bergson's doctrines concerning space and time in-

volve a revelation of certain uncriticized assumptions made

by Kant, one of which has already been mentioned, viz. the

legitimacy of spatializing time.  It is the criticism of

this assumption, among others, that leads Bergson to go be-

yond Kant in his theory of space and time.  It may be said,

however, that Bergson might well have criticized other as-

sumptions than those he did.  He might, for example, if he

had been a philosopher of a different persuasion, have cri-

ticized the way in which Kant distinguishes between space

and time and have modified Kant's views in the direction of

a manifold theory which excluded passage.  It may be that a

theory of space-time which excludes passage will prove to

be the most defensible theory.  We suggest, however, that

at present this is far from being obvious, and that cogent

reasons seem to point to the opposite conclusion.  At any

rate, Bergson's criticism did not take this line of depar-

ture, and for this reason we do not here deal with that con-

tingency.  But more essentially, it is felt as well that such

a modification of Kant does not represent a logical development

of Kant's theory of space and time, but rather a clean break
with it in the for  of an entirely different view of space
and time.  For in one way at least,  ant was making no un-
critical assumption in drawing a fundamental distinction between space and time.  He shows himself to  ave been conscious
 of the most i portant reasons for doing so, particularly
in his exa ination of the relation between time and inner
sense.  Kant's theory of space and time is intimately bound
up with his own conception of the critical philosophy as he
conceived it, and it is the relation of this position to
that of Bergson that we consider.  ith re ard to the question of the extent to which the critical philosophy may be
modified so as to be compatible with a theory of space-time
which denies the fun amental uniqueness of time, and still
retain the essentials of the critical position, we male no
commitment, except that which we have already indicated,
namely, that such a modification will, in some respects, be
un-Kantian.  The respects in which we  aintain it will be
so, pertain, within the scope of this thesis only to the
theory of space and time.  e do not intend to su  est that
all aspects of  ant's thou ht, or even the essential aspects
of it, necessarily involve his funcamental distinction between space and time.

Nor do we wish to pass judg ent on the relative merits
of Kant's position as it stands in his writings or on the
possibility of a renovated Kantianism which would involve

the obsolescence of Kant's distinction.  In connection with
this, however, it may be said that it is not entirely obvious that because modern physics requires a theory of space-
time, Kant's position, if it is to be defensible in the light
of the new physics, needs to be changed in a manner which
would obliterate his way of distinguishing between space and
time.  This is, itself, a difficult and extensive problem,
and like the others mentioned above, lies outside the particular subject we wish to explore.  We take Kant's position
on space and time as he expressed it, and consider only the
developments from a position which retains that specific
character, that is, from a position which involves a fundamental distinction between space and time.  Thus, when we
speak of logical development, we mean development of the
metaphysical implications of a theory.  The theory which we
are dealing with is one which includes the premise that time
is ultimately and uniquely different from space.  And the
reason why we treat of development in this sense is that we
feel that there are sound reasons for making this basic distinction.

Finally, it is advisable to sum up the similarities
between Kant and Bergson, which constitute the main <u>raisons
d'être</u> of this thesis.  The importance which both philosophers attach to their views of space and time is worth no-
ting.  Bergson's views concerning the relationship between

space and time lie at the base of his metaphysics. Kant'
Transcend ntal Aesthetic stands in the foreground of his
philosop y as an absoluvely indispensable part of it. Th
position of neither philosopher can be u derstood without
comprehension of his doctrine  of space and time.

But the resemblance between ant and Ber son need
not be limited to generalities. This is particularly true
of their views on space a d ti e. Both, as we have alrea
emphasized, make a fundamental distinction between space
and time, and for both this distinction has a considerabl
if not decisive, bearing on how they work out other parts
of their philosophies. In addition, both philosophers re
gard inner experience as highly important in connection
with the apprehension of time. Both hold that time canno
be represented directly, but only through the mediation o
space. They agree that space is uniquely associated with
the logical functions of the understanding. Both call att
tion to the all-pervasiveness of time, in contradistincti
to spatiality. And both are faced with the problems whic
the distinction between space and time poses. It is thes
problems which lead Bergson to a theory w'ich can be regarded as a development of Kant's views, and which allow
him to draw out the implications of Kant's mode of distin
guishing between space and time in a manner which Kant,
himself did not envisage. In this respect, only one furth

point of clarification concerning our subject needs to be
made. This is that while there undoubtedly are historica
connections n' influe ces betveen ant an  er son, our
treat nt is  eant to be systematic rather t an  istorica
The relations we exa ine between the two men  ay or may n
be paralleled in point of historical connection. For the
most part, they probably are not.
6

## CHAPTER TWO

PRELIMINARY DISCUSSION OF THE DISTINCTION
BETWEEN SPACE AND TIME

## 1.  General Features of the Distinction between
Space and Time

No distinction is more familiar to common sense and
more difficult to give a philosophic account of than the
distinction between space and time.  In everyday experience
we are not often confused as to what is spatial and what is
temporal.  But in philosophy, some questions which we can
ask about the world seem to demand that we give some account
of the separation between space and time, and indicate how,
or in what sense, we know them to be fundamentally different.

If, for example, we ask ourselves whether all things
exist in space and time, or whether some exist in one and
not the other, or in neither, we find it difficult to put
forth an answer without committing ourselves to some view
concerning the different natures of space and time.  We may,
of course, in answering such questions reach the conclusion
that it is a mistake to regard space and time as fundamentally different, and this will have an important bearing on
the kind of answers we give.  Even if we take the position
that it is futile to attempt to inquire into the "nature"
of such things, and concern ourselves simply with the way

h spaces and times are measured, we have not removed
essity of deciding in what sense they are distinguish-
For we do in fact measure them differently, and this
onstitutes a recognition of a difference between them.

Once any basis of distinction is accepted, the quest-
ses as to whether this basis is adequate to the ex-
on of all aspects of the distinction between space
e, and whether it is compatible with the similarities
them.  We have then to take account of the different
which space and time are viewed in the various spe-
iences.

The different ways in which space is regarded in
tics and in psychology is well expressed by Cassirer.

If from the standpoint of metageometry, Eucli-
an geometry appears as a mere beginning, as given
terial for further developments, nevertheless, from
e standpoint of the critique of knowledge, it re-
esents the end of a complicated series of intellectual
erations.  The psychological investigations of the
igin of the idea of space (including those which were
dertaken with a purely sensationalistic tendency)
ve indirectly confirmed and clarified this. They
ow unmistakably that the space of our sense percep-
on is not identical with the space of our geometry,
t is distinguished from it in exactly the decisive
nstitutive properties.  "Above" and "below", "right"
d "left" are here not equivalent directions, which
n be exchanged with each other without change, but
ey remain qualitatively distinct and irreducible
terminations, since totally different groups of or-
nic sensations correspond to them.  In geometrical
ace, on the contrary, all these oppositions are can-
lled.  8

Similarly, the difference between time as it appears
hology and as it appears in physics, has been stressed

by Gunn, who states that "Neither psychology nor physics attempts to grasp the problem of the nature of time in its full significance; the one is merely concerned with our subjective awareness of time and the other confines itself largely to considerations of measurement".[9] Gunn points out some of the differences between time as it is dealt with in these two contexts.

> For instance, time as perceived is always limited. We never perceive the whole of time. It is also perceived as sensibly continuous, as having a certain directional quality; it is transitive and related in its content to the subject at the moment of experience. Only if the wider _implied_ temporal perspective and the time-span immediately experienced be apprehended as passing into one another can Time be grasped, and in this way it is grasped as a continuum. Time as conceived is unlimited in character, is regarded as infinitely divisible and mathematically continuous like an infinite series. Further, it is looked on as involving an objective order of before-and-after, which is not to be equated with the past, present or future of a subject. . . Conceptual time is also conceived to be a unity in spite of the difficulty of ascribing to it any principle of coherence. Perceptual time, however, is rooted in experience and professions of unity are not to be made in regard to it. There may on this level be many unrelated times. [10]

Until quite recent times the distinction between space and time, whatever it may turn out to involve on closer inspection, has been carried over from common sense into the special sciences, in general, without much modification. Indeed, to common sense the distinction seems to be so obvious that the question of whether or not space and time are distinct seems to be irrelevant. Were it not for the merging, in contemporary physics, of physical space and physical

time in a space-time continuum, and for a similar merging
of space and time in recent metaphysical theories,[11] one might
rest content in the view that they are distinct, and direct
one's attention to grasping the peculiar nature of each.
They offer perplexities enough when taken separately. We
have Minkowski's famous statement, however, and its repetition by numerous popular expositors, to remind us that it
would be rash to assume uncritically that space and time at
least in the context of physics are ultimate and distinct.

> The views of space and time which I wish to
> lay before you have sprung from the soil of experimen-
> tal physics, and therein lies their strength. They
> are radical. Henceforth space by itself, and time by
> itself, are doomed to fade away into mere shadows, and
> only a kind of union of the two will preserve an inde-
> pendent reality. [12]

Yet Minkowski's prediction seems to have been pre-
mature. Another eminent physicist expresses a more moderate
estimate of the effect of the space-time conception on the
physical distinction between space and time.

> Although mathematical attempts to demonstrate
> the unity of space and time in a single four-dimensional
> world do not completely obliterate the difference be-
> tween distances and durations, they certainly reveal
> a much greater similarity between the two notions than
> was ever evident in pre-Einsteinian physics. [13]

Thus the question arises as to whether space and
time are ultimately or fundamentally distinct; and if so,
in what their distinction consists. It is not merely that
we do constantly distinguish them in everyday life. It is
also a question of whether those aspects of experience which

w  desi n .to  s space and time are si.iple and irreducible,
each incapable of further explanation in terms of something
else; or whether they admit of analysis into more basic elements in t r is of which their very difference in experience
would be explained.  In either case, it is apparent that we
are faced with a philosophic problem rather than a purely
physical or psychological problem.  Physics, at least in its
present form, says nothing about how the space-time continuum
is related to the psychological apprehension of space and
time; nor does the science of psychology relate its views
to those of physics.

It can be agreed, of course, that the accounts of
the distinction between space and time given by the special
sciences, the expositions, that is, of what each is "known
as", cannot be ignored by the philosopher who wishes to know
whether they are ultimately distinct or not.  For he is not
merely setting out to give one more particular account of
space and time, but is concerned to give an explanation which
will embody the results of the particular sciences, either
in the sense of showing one or more of them to be in error,
and _how_ such error comes about, or in the sense of incorporating scientific results into a more general theory.

Such a general theory of space and time may be either
monistic or dualistic depending on whether it takes the view
that space and time are _not_ ultimately distinct, or the view

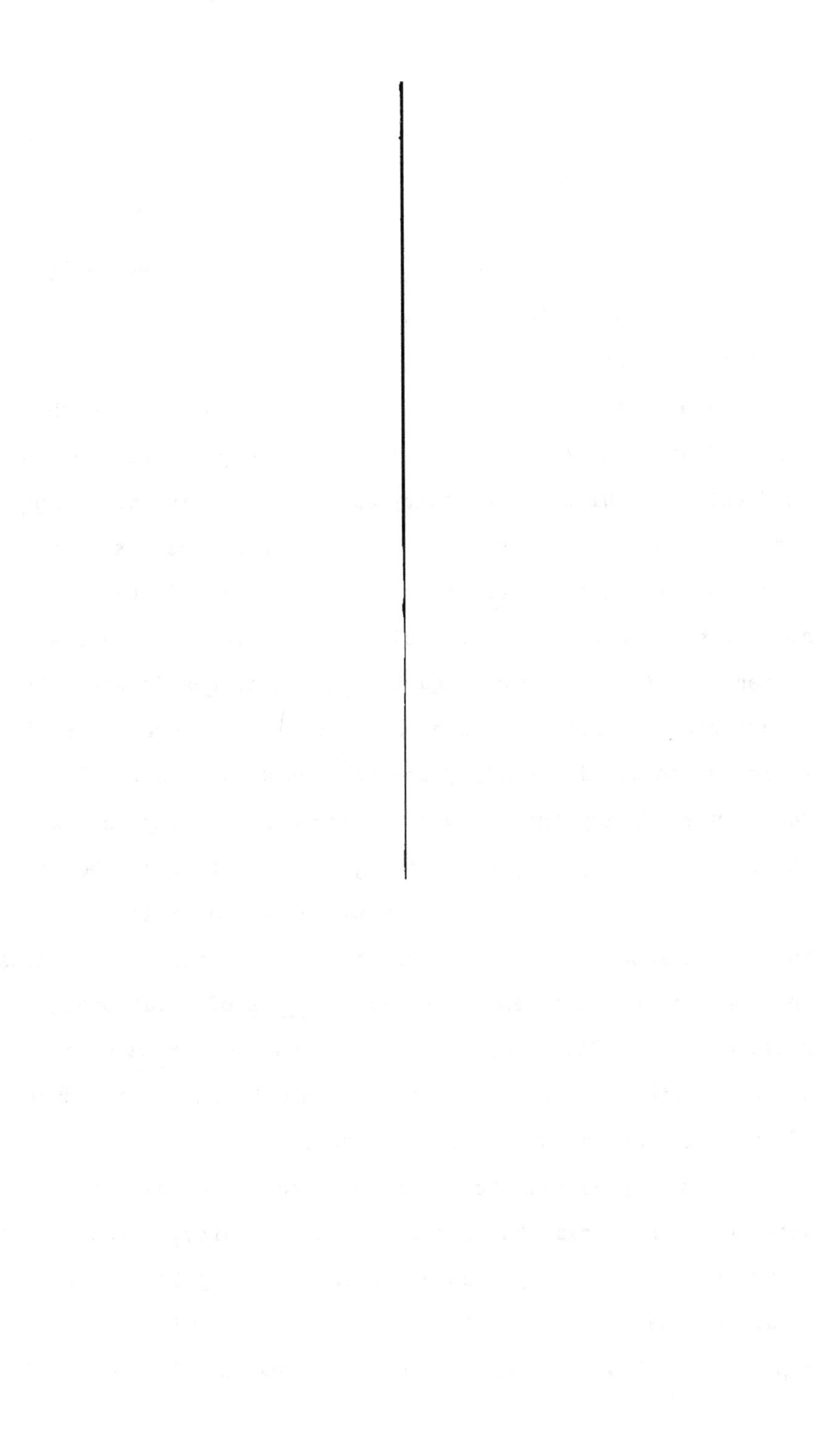

that they are.  In either case, it will be necessary to take
into consideration the way in which space and time are distinguished in different sciences.  But it is just here that
t'e greatest difficulty arises.  If it is supposed that they
are ultimately distinct, it will not be enough merely to re-
cord this.  It will be necessary also to state in what _manner_
they are distinct, or in other words, in what the distinction
consists.  Are both space and time to be placed in the category of that which is immediately intuited in sensible experience?  Are they to be regarded as atomic qualia exhibited
in experience?  Are they to be construed as different formal
wholes which are logically prior to spatial and temporal
relations?  Or may they be distinguished by placing one in
the realm of the purely conceptual, and the other as the content of a peculiar kind of non-intellectual intuition?  Are
they to be interpreted as different self-subsisting substances?
Or  are they ultimate and irreducible _kin_s of relations?
These are some of the ways in which space and time may be
basically distinguished.  For all of them there are a number
of crucial problems which must be faced.

A metaphysical theory of space and time must take
account of the claim that experience has a unity,  either
in the sense of denying such unity or accepting it.  If it
be agreed that human experience presupposes a unifying principle, it follows that spatio-temporal aspects of that

experience must reflect that principle. That is, there must
be a unity, in some sense, of space and time. How that unity
is possible, considering the intrinsic difference between
space and time, is a question of first importance. It will
not be a problem for a philosopher who repudiates any fundamental distinction between space and time. But for one
who accepts a distinction it will be crucial.

What, then, are the problems which such a philosopher must try to solve? For purposes of illustration, let
us consider the view that space and time are distinct substances.[14] This theory brings certain difficulties into sharp
focus, for it places them in the context of the traditional
problem of how one substance can act upon, or be related to
another substance. The concept of substance as that which
exists in itself is peculiarly obdurate to relatedness.
Spinoza's addition to the traditional definition, namely,
that a substance is also that which is conceived through
itself,[15] clarifies the nature of these difficulties. For
a substance _qua_ substance, (i.e. _not qua_ accident), has,
according to its definition, nothing in com on with any other
substance, and hence two such substances cannot be mutually
understood.[16] Now how two such substances can have any sort
of relation, capable of being known, is indeed a perplexing
question. It is possible that they might be related in a
fashion which cannot be known, that is, in a fashion which

cannot be un erstood, but must be grasped, if at all, through
means other tl an co niition.  (This is an important possibility
and has an obvious affinity to Bergson's doctrine of  eta-
physical intuition).  The crux of the puzzle is that two
substances must h ve somtl in  in common, or must resemble
one another in some  ay, in order to be mutually understood,
qua substance,  and they cannct, by definition, have anything
in com on.  It i ht vell be said that it is the definition
of substance which is at fault, and should therefore be dis-
carded, but since ve are here concerned only vith substance
in the cont xt of an illustration, we leave that objection
to one side.  For the importance of substance for our present purposes lies not in any question of the usefulness of
substance for philosophy, but in the illustration of the
difficulties of cognizing relatedness.  Considered from this
point of view, the old problem concerning the relations of
two substances, comes to be seen as the problem of knowing
two things which have not ing in common, and this applies,
not merely to substances, but to anything whatever that we
are acquainted with.  If we become acquainted with anything
which literally has not ing in cor on with anything else we
are acquainted with, the possibility of cognizing it is ruled
out.  /e can be said to know it only if ve consider it permissible to speak of knowledge by acquaintance in the manner
of Russell,  [17] and this is a different sense of the term "knowledge" from the one we are considering at the moment.

## 23

Knowledge by acquaintance of something which has
nothing in common with anything else, however, will not carry
us very far in explaining the world, for we cannot relate
such knowledge to anything else, except accidentally, or a
posteriori.  Whatever else it may be, such knowledge is not
the kind which metaphysicians have traditionally sought. About
all we can do with an entity which has nothing in common
with anything else is to designate it by a proper name.  It
might be said that in naming it we endow it with one common
property at least, viz., that of being in the class of things
which may be spoken of.  But this ignores the fact that whatever name we give it is not intrinsic to the thing, not an
essential attribute without which the thing would not exist,
but is merely accidental and unessential.  By naming it we
do not relate it necessarily to anything else, for our name
does not imply that there is anything common between the entity and something else.  It is only when we can form a concept of a thing which contains something in with the concept
of another thing, that we can have rational knowledge of the
two.  And in this case, of course, the very fact that we can
conceptualize a thing in terms of common properties, means
that the thing is not unique.

It may well be asked whether there are any such absolutely unique entities, or alternatively, whether everything with which we are acquainted is absolutely unique.  We

...ay put this question in other terms and ask whether we ever
do have concepts, in terms of common properties, of things
with which we are acquainted, or whether our concepts, in
their generality, always allow the intrinsic uniqueness of
things to escape. And this amounts to asking whether anything we are acquainted with resembles anything else. This,
it should be noted, is a point of a different order from
the truism that general concepts, in their generality, leave
certain aspects of the objects conceptualized unspecified.
If it be admitted that describing something in general terms
omits its particularity, it is an easy step to the position that there is in the universe a principle of the undetermined, which remains over when conceptualization has
done its work, and might be suitably spoken of as "that which
in itself is not a 'this'". If concepts leave a residue,
the residue must be conceptually undetermined. This position,
interesting as it is in itself, is not the one we are concerned with here. What we are concerned with is the possibility that there may be entities which are absolutely
unique, and not amenable to any sort of conceptualization.
With reference to the majority of objects of experience, we
may feel sure that the question answers itself, for we undoubtedly are aware of numerous resemblances between things.
If we relate this question to space and time, however, we
seem to be less certain of the answer, and several possibilities present themselves.

## 25

First, we may take the view that our concepts of
space and time are adequate to their objects. This raises
the question of whether our concepts of space and time have
anything in common and whether they have, together, anything
in common with anything else. This view involves the question
of whether, in dealing with space and time, we are dealing
with two unique entities, or whether we are forming discursive concepts of spatiality and temporality, that is, whether we are bringing under single concepts of space and time,
a plurality of spaces and times, respectively. For Kant,
of course, the process of conceptualization always involves
the bringing of particulars under one concept. He does not
use the term "concept", except for the occasional slip, in
a manner which implies that we could have a concept of something absolutely unique. And he rejects the view that space
and time are discursive concepts.

Secondly, we may take the view, with Kant, that space
and time are not concepts. This means that they are entities
which are absolutely unique. We cannot conceive them in
terms of properties which they have in common with other entities. For if they have anything in common with something
else, they can be conceptualized. It should be added that
we are speaking here of the intrinsic properties of space
and time. In so far as we cannot form concepts of the intrinsic natures of space and time, we must admit that they
are absolutely unique entities.

Regarding the distinction between space and time, we have, then, four main possibilities, which may be ordered as follows:

1. Space and time are adequately represented by discursive concepts which have nothing in common.

2. Space and time are adequately represented by discursive concepts which have something in common.

3. Space and time are not representable by concepts, but are unique particulars with which we can be acquainted.

4. Either space or time (but not both) is representable by a concept.

There is, of course, a fifth possibility, which could be expressed as follows: "Neither space nor time is representable by a concept and neither of them is an entity with which we can be acquainted". This would be the view of those (e.g. Vaihinger) who hold that space and time are 'fictions". But since this position is remote from the views of both Kant and Bergson, we need not discuss it further.

From the point of view of maintaining a fundamental distinction between space and time, the first of the above possibilities offers obvious difficulties. These are analogous to the difficulties concerning the relation between two substances, which we have mentioned. If space and time are adequately represented by concepts and these concepts have nothing whatever in common, we should never be able to

conceive of any relation between the two.  Ie could never have a rational knowledge of how space and time are related, for example, in the phenomenon of motion.  If this were, indeed, the case, it would be a highly undesirable state of affairs from the point of view of human knowledge.  For although we could understand space and time by themselves, our knowledge of the world would display these two unrelated aspects, and so create a dualism which we could never resolve.  It should be added that if space and time are not representable by concepts, we should not expect to have a rational knowledge of their relations.  But if they are representable by concepts, we should, in metaphysics, expect to have rational knowledge of their mutual relations.  But if these concepts have nothing in common, this expectation would be frustrated.  This would seem all the more intolerable just because we were able to <u>conceive</u> space and time, by themselves, adequately.  Knowledge would be bifurcated; motion and change would be inexplicable.

The second possibility represents a denial of any fundamental or intrinsic distinction between space and time. For it is clear that if the intrinsic or essential natures of space and time have something in common, we can form a concept of the essential nature which will represent the essential nature of <u>both</u> space and time.  A single concept will be adequate to represent what is essential in both

space and time.  Extensiveness, perhaps, would fulfill the
requirements of such a concept.  This second possibility is,
in fact, the one taken by those who uphold the theory of the
manifold.  Since this position will be examined in detail
below, we leave it aside here, except to remark that the
question of what is essential to space and time, and whether
space and time may both be represented by concepts is a
highly debatable one.

It is immediately apparent that if we choose the
third possibility, we rule out the possibility that space
and time resemble one another.  For if they resembled one
another, they would not be unique entities, and the second
of the first two possibilities would be true.  In other words,
in choosing the third possibility, we make a fundamental
distinction between space and time.  In this case we cannot
expect to be able to <u>understand</u> the relation between space
and time, although we may well be able to become acquainted
with it through some other means.  The extent of our understanding of the relation between space and time will be to
point out that they do not resemble one another and cannot
be conceived in terms of one another.  The metaphysical implications of this position are as startling in their way
as are those of the first possibility.  According to this
view, space and time are simply two unique entities which
we may meet with in the course of experience, having no

conceivable relation to each ot.er or co anyt ing else.  In
view of the indubitable fact tlat space  id time are among
the most .ervasive aspects of oui experience, this view
would be stra..ge indeed.  It seems s all coifort to note
that the relation between space and cime would seem, on this
view, no nore inexplicaole than space and tiie themselves.
The task of metaphysics, here, would simply be to point out
this staue of affairs, and to attempt, perhaps, through the
non-cognitive functions of language to communicate sonething
of the _feel_ of ultimate irrationalities.  Metaphysics could
proceed only in a manner quite unlike the metaphysics which
attempts to give an account of the rational structure of
the world.

The fourth possioility offers .ore scope to the intellect.  Here either space or t..ie will be considered to be
adequacely represented by means of concepts, while the re-
maining one will be considered an intrinsically unique entity, which escanes conceptualization.  That Bergson's philosophy falls under t'is possibility can easily be seen.  For
he considers space to be conceptualizable but time not.  The
other alternative of taking space as a unique entity and
leaving tiie to the intellect, would have the rather unplau-
sible result that geometry would have nothing to do with
space, however accurately it might be held to represent temporal determinations.  Within this fourth possibility,

Ber son's c' ice see s to be t' e obvious on . Nevertheless,
the  i  t i   ot  o obvious as to be  as ed  it' out argument.  e s'all, t' erefore, in subsequent cha ters, present
Bergson's arguments on this  oint, and the relation of  is
views to those of Kant.

It will be ap arent fro  t' e fore oin  that a theory
w' ich deals with the  roblem of the fundamental distinction
between s ace and time must take one of the four possibilities
listed above.  Since neit' er Kant nor Bergson thinks of <u>both</u>
space and time as adequately representable in concepts, possibility one is not useful for our pur oses.  So we shall dis-
regard it.  Possibility two represents a view opposed to any
intrinsic distinction between space and time.  And since Kant
and Bergson both wish to maintain such a distinction, this
possibility can also be eliminated from our discussion.  It
should be added that neither of possibilities one and two can
represent Kant's views, since he re eatedly emphasizes that
space and time are not concepts.  There remain, then, possibilities three and four which  rovide the general means w' ereby
Kant and Bergson might explain t' e distinction between space
and time.  It will be observed t' at,  ithin these limitations,
<u>at least one</u> of space and time must be recognized as a unique
entity not adequately representable by means of concepts.
It follows,  oreover, that for a philosopher  ho holds that
geometry is ap licable to,  nd indeed, requires an intuition

of, space, it will not be possible to maintain that space
is that unique entity which absolutely eludes conceptualization.

within possibilities three and four, there is room,
however, for a certain amount of eclecticism.  Space, for
example, might be considered to be a unique entity, but ana-
lysable in terms of intrinsic, derivative properties, which
are represented by concepts pertaining to spatiality, the
discursive concept of space.  This would involve the doctrine
that the plurality of spaces, from which the concept of spatiality is derived, are parts of the one unique entity, space.
As a whole it would be impossible to form a concept of space,
for there would be nothing else like it, which it could resemble.  There would be no properties common to space as a
whole and to something else, which would allow us to form a
concept.  There would be nothing to prevent us, however,
from forming a concept of spatiality from the common properties of a plurality of the <u>parts</u> of space.  And in so far as
what is true of the parts of a homogeneous medium is true
of the whole, our knowledge of spatiality would be true also
of space, even though we could not directly have a concept
of it.  But such eclecticism will have sharp limits.  It
would not be possible to carry out the same procedure for
both space and time.  That is, it would not be possible to
say of both space and time that they were unique entities,

but both capable of being adequately represented in terms of concepts which have any property in common, for example, that of extensiveness or divisibility. An eclecticism of possibilities one and three might be possible if it could be shown that the intrinsic properties of time had nothing in common with those of space. But if it were supposed that possibilities two and three could be combined, this would involve a clear contradiction. For such a view would be committed to saying that space and time were unique entities which had nothing in common, but could be adequately represented by concepts which had something essential to space and time in common. For this reason, we have not listed this supposition as a legitimate possibility.

It might be objected to the above scheme that it narrows the available metaphysical possibilities to the point of absurdity. In one sense only, this is true, and the sense in which it is true, that we have narrowed down the possibilities, is, we maintain, not absurd. The principle we have accepted is this: that either time is essentially similar to space or it is not. And we confess to having enough faith in the law of excluded middle to hold this proposition true, simply as a matter of logic.

To sum up, then, a metaphysical account of the distinction between space and time must take one of the three possibilities we have indicated, or some permissible eclectic

combination of them.  It must, in a dition, take account of the way in w ich space and time are distinguished in the special sciences.  ith reference to the latter requirement, it will be nec ssary to state in what the distinction con- sists.

To return to our original point of departure, the question of the unity of experience, it can be seen that the above poss ble ways of distinguishing between space and time impose conditions on the possible ans ers to this question. If, for example, it is held that space and time are not re- present ble by concepts, and yet it is also held, as Kant seems to do, that experience exhibits a spatio-temporal unity, it will clearly be impossible to give a rational account of this unity.  The question of what relations between space and time can be conceived, will, in term s of this position, be meaningless.  The question of how space and time come to be united in one nature must ret ain unanswered.  The further question of how two unique entities, which do not admit of a common conceptual representation, can be represented in terms of one another will likewise be unanswerable.  Also, how it is possible that elements of experience which are in time alone, can be spoken of and represented in terms which are appropriate to spatial elements, will be a problem which will be impossible to resolve.  We shall find that

se are questions of a kind which    nt, in accordance with
dictates of his position, gives no answers.

## 35

## 2. <u>Similarities and Differences between Space and Time</u>

The analogous properties of space and time were no-
ticed by Locke, who distinguished space and time as two distinct, simple ideas.

> To conclude: expansion and duration do mutually
> embrace and comprehend each other; every part of space
> being in every part of duration, and every part of du-
> ration in every part of expansion. Such a combination
> of two distinct ideas, is, I suppose, scarce to be found
> in all that great variety we do or can conceive, and
> may afford matter to farther speculation. 18

Locke would have been amazed, perhaps, to know how
far speculation in this regard has been carried out since
his day. The mathematical treatment of space and time provides a conspicuous example of the emphasis on the similarities between space and time. Without committing oneself to
the doctrine that space and time as they are dealt with mathematically in physical science constitute, without qualification, what space and time are, it is possible, nevertheless, to maintain the philosophic importance of their similarity in this context. Whatever theory is adopted on the
question of whether they are ultimately distinct or not, the
mathematical treatment of space and time cannot be ignored.
One of the strongest arguments in favour of this view is the
indubitable success of the mathematical treatment in allowing
predictions to be made concerning spatio-temporal events in
the world. Yet it should be noted that this point does not
necessarily involve the view that space and time are ultimately

or intrinsically similar.  Whitehead's theory of space and
time provides an interesting example of how it may be possible to uphold a fundamental distinction between space and
time, while taking advantage of the mathematical treatment
of them through their analogous properties.  In his criticism
of classical physics, Whitehead at the same time grants the
success of its methods, even though, for him, they create
philosophic problems which demand reconsideration of the entire concept of nature.

> We cannot wonder that science rested content with
> this assumption as to the fundamental elements of nature.
> The great forces of nature, such as gravitation, were en-
> tirely determined by the configurations of masses.  Thus
> the circle of scientific thought was completely closed.
> This is the famous mechanistic theory of nature, which
> has reigned supreme ever since the seventeenth century.
> It is the orthodox creed of physical science.  Further-
> more the creed justified itself by the pragmatic test.
> It worked.  19

Whitehead saw clearly that part of the success of
this theory was due to its taking advantage of a common feature of space and time.  This allowed a conception of matter
as having the property of simple location, which Whitehead
explains as "one major characteristic which refers equally
both to space and to time, and other minor characteristics
which are diverse as between space and time". [20]  He explains
this common feature as follows:

## 37

The ch racteristic co. on both to space and time is t'at material can be s.id to be _lor_ in s ace and _.ere_ in time, or _here_ in space-time, in a perfectly _efinite sense vi ich does not require for its expl.nation any re-f.rence to other re ions of space-ti e. Curiously enough t is ch r cter stic of si. le location ol s whetl r we look on a region of space-time as determined absolutely or rel tively. 21

White ead consi ers t.e assum tion of the simple lo-cation of matter to be a fallacy if it is taken to express a philosophical trut . about the world. At best t e ass'' ption is an abstr ction wl ich mathe atics is eminently capable of expressin .

.l e seventeent'. century had finally produced a scheme of sci ntific thou ht fr ed by r athematicians, for t e use of mathematicians. The _reat characteristic of the mathematical mind is its capacity for dealing vith abs rac ions; and for eliciting _rom them clear-cut demonstrative chains of reasoning, entirely satis-factory so lo ig as it is a tr ctions wI ich you want to think about. The enormous success of the scientific ab-stractions, yielding on the one hand _matter_ with its _simple location_ ih space and time, on the other hand _mind_, perceiv ig, suf ering, reasonin , but not inter-ferin , has foisted onto philosophy the task of accepting the is the ost concrete r nderin of _ ct. 22

What mat' e atics is concerned with, however, is "the investiga on of patterns of connect dness, in abs r ction from the particular relata and t particular ode of con-23 nection". It is not surprising, t erefor , to find aspects of space and ti e, in hitehead's philoso hy coalescing in a space-ti e continuum under o e gui e of their com on charac-ter as extensive r lations. Yet hitehea maintains n ulti-mate distinction between space and ti e. In their co on

c'aracter of extensity, s.ac  n      re  a      .o.en of
 "t'c extens_v, c itin  '.  ut,    i  ~ not  roce ' to
conceive ti.e as an t' r ? m ef exue.r ven  s'  hite ead
realizes .io clea-ly , , t.c conc ju o' sp re-.i e, conceived as a .l work cf relations, obliterates the distinction
between space .id ti.e.

  u. 'is exhi..itio. uf t e actual i iverse as
extensive  nd divisible has left out t e distinction
bet.een s.ac  .nd tu. e.  25

 f'er. is a way out  f .is difficulty.  .at'er.tics,
which  eals  ith the extensive continuu.., involves only external rel tions, a'str.ct d fro. t . rel .a.  f.e rel.ta in
corcrete nature are <u>inte.m.lly</u> relaued.  _ .s .n 'e .o.crete,
internally rel.ted events of nature that act al ti. e is .ani-
fested.

 Whiter.ad's .re . nt of . .ce .n t. e .ll s.m .tes
the a.p asis on their a. l.,. s .ro.r .es fr.  t.e st.d-
point of p.re r.la.ion, .nd .n a .iti n ..a.s hov t. se .ra-
lo ies ma. be  ealt .it. in .et p.y.ics .u.out thereby ex-
plain.n  avay . r..l dil..renc. 'et . n s.ac. .n. .i. e.  It
is not to .he pr s.nt purpose to  iscuss t e partic.lar . .n-
ner .n w. ic. hitchead .s .cco pli..ed t.is .eat, .ut erely
to point out that he sav tl.e reces.ity of doi..g .o.  .his is
all the . ore inter.sting .n t'.t 'ite.e .'s acco .t of the
analogous properties of space  .d ti..e, partic.larly .n .is
early vor..s, is stron_ly in.lue.c.d by  .s conc..tic.. of

...te tics s   _  1 scie ce ˜p    _ tions.   _  ana-
lo˜i_s for    ec e  r l  h,i_,    _s s ch turn out
not to b  _ilo i_s at all c˜ f.   _  l_ _iffer_t e.tities,
_t  re r_l_c d _y o._ relational co plex, t _ exten_ive con-
_inuu , _ ic _cous _t_tes all t e sp _ic-_o _oral relacio_s
_et_ee_ c_ic__u_ occasio_s. _his is a r_ther diff_rent _e_od
o_ _tt_ck fro_ _l_at of _ _  _ _ mathe avic _ wh_, i_ _e cares
to,  a su_dy _t_ _._ec_s o_ _ ose rela_ions _su__ly ac_now-
lea_ed to _._ c _ ct__istic of _ime, _nd t_ose us _lly ac_no_-
led_od t_ b_ characteris_ic __ _ _c_, se__r_ely, _it_out
_ec__s_rily co _i_t_ _g_hi self _s _c__aed er_ _ese r_la_ions
_s exe_olified i_ p_e_o_na _f_e _ o_e co_l_ _hole. It is,
ho_ever, _n _n__r__u_d_ble s_ep to t_e, _n_ _y, p_rh_ps,
_e _he only pos_io_e o_e _f _ _e _a__e._ical _re __ _t o_
_pace _nd _i_e is to _e _ _o_ ser_ousl_.

It is i_teres_i_ _o _o_e  _u _  r _ _l, _owev_r,
that fro_ _ne stand_oi_t of _ur_ _eo__ry _ne f_sion of s_ace
_nd ti_e _ay _ __ _la_e i_ ei_he_ o_ _o_ _ays. Geom_ri_s
_ased o_ rel_t_o_s _a__t _o _e c__r c_erist_c _f _ ysic l
space _ay _nco__or_te _i_e as _ four_h di_ension; or relations charac_eristic of _i_o __y_ _ consi __ _ _o be _r_or,
_nd relati_ns ch r_cter_s_ic of _pace _a_ _e _eriv_d fro_
t_o_. _t least, __ o_e case, _n a__e_pt _a_ _een __e to
_uil_ up _ _eo_etr_ of four _i_e_sio_s _f _i_e _n_ re_ _ired
_y _heoret__cal phy_sics, fro_ _he rel_tio_s o_ <u>before</u> _nd

[illegible] after, which [illegible] in [illegible]

[illegible]

[illegible], so to
speak, swimming along in an ocean of space (as we usually do), we [illegible] either as some-
how pursuing a course in an ocean of time; while spacial
relations [illegible] regarded as the manifestation of the
fact that the elements of time form a system in conical
order: [illegible] in terms of
the relations of before and after. 26

The author of this geometry builds it up by a formal
procedure of deducing theorems from postulates: "The geometry
as I have pointed out is a logical structure built up from
certain postulates which I shall formulate". 27 Thus, if this
author has been successful, it would seem that relations taken
to be characteristic of space need not, from the mathematical
point of view, be considered to be fundamental. We need not,
in the words of C. J. Broad, ". . .talk, or listen to, nonsense about 'Time being a fourth dimension of Space'", 28 even
in the context of mathematics.

What, then are the analogous properties of space and
time, and where does the analogy which they suggest break off?
In addition to one characteristic to which Whitehead has drawn
attention, namely, that we can speak meaningfully of a "here"
in time as well as in space, there are a group of properties
which are thought to be common to both space and time, and
which have often been referred to as their "extensiveness".
C. D. Broad sums up these characteristics in an illustration

d i l o              ti     e  x   v   s ect of ti e.

                            n         o ce ve    ong
events are similar to the relations of  artial or co plete
overl  in  ic      re i  i      e of two ex-
te ded ob ec  , li e a pair of sticks.  he possiole time-
r l t             evn  s    bo c  l tely r  resented
by ta in  a single straight line, lett   'left-to-ri ht"
on t is s   l for 'e rlier  nd later',  n  t  ing two
stretches on this line to represent a pair of finite
ev    .  2)

   i  , li e space, s  ms to   it of quantic tiv  de-

termiinti ns.  his  s al o brou ht out b  Locke, who, al-

t ou   he r  arded space  nd ti e as t o distinct ideas,

t ou ht t  t t ey i ht  e  ore clearly  nd distinctly  nown

if t ey  re co  red with one a other.

            Ir  ot  of t ese (viz.    asio  an  uration)
t e  ind has this com on i ea of continued lengths, ca-
   ole of  re ter or less quantities; for a  an has  s
clear an idea of the difference of the len th of an hour
and  day a  of an i c  a d a foot.  30

     Loc e  lso tc ches u on ot  r as ects of the exten-

siver ss of     nd ti e,  ic  ave t eir counterparts in

Proad's re resenttion.  or ex  le, Loc e says that " ll

t e parts of  xt nsion  re extens on,   all the p rts of

duration  re  uration"; in ot er vor s, sp ce  nd ti e in
31

t eir character of extensiveness  re homo eneous.  Two f r-

ther co  on properties of t e exten iver ess of space  nd time

are  entioned by Loc e.  e    i fluenced by  e ton's theory

of a solute space  n  ti e, he emph  sizes t at both space and

ti e c  be conceiv d of as inf  ite.  x ansion is not bounded

by  a ter, nor durat on by  otion, but each  ay be thought of

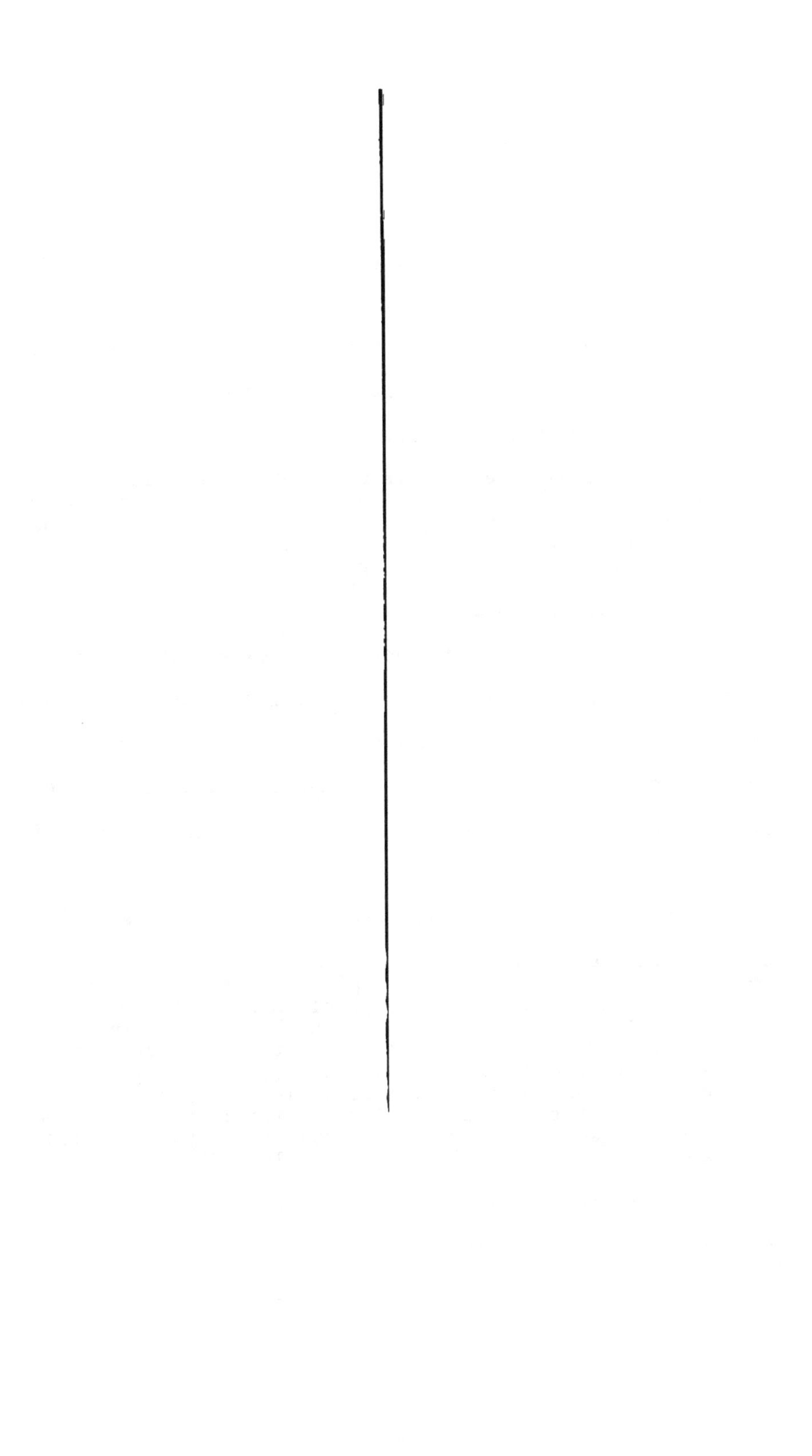

... ertain, but the idea of a particular one th or one or
the other had been seized upon.

corollary to the infinite extension of space and
time, Locke is that they admit of finite determination,
that is, they are divisible into particular lengths.

Time in general is to duration as place to expansion. They are so chief of those boundless oceans of
eternity and immensity, as is set out and distinguished
from the rest as it were land marks; as also are they
used of to denote the position of finite real beings, in
respect to one another, in those uniform infinite oceans
of duratio and space. 32

All of these general aspects of extensiveness, viz.
homo eneity, divisibility, the possibility of infinite extension, and simple location, may be regarded as analogous
properties of space and time. Whether strict adherence to
such a view is defensible in the final analysis, however, is
another question. Emphasis on these properties, as Broad
points out, is apt to obscure the very real difference between space and time.

At first sight the problems of time look very
much like those of space, except that the single dimension of Time, as compared with the three of Space,
seems to promise greater simplicity. We shall point
out these analogies at the beginning; but we shall
find that they are somewhat superficial, and that time
and Change are extremely difficult subjects, in which
spatial analogies help us but little. 33

If space and time are looked upon as certain kinds
of relations exhibited in experience, the differences between
them become evident. The successiveness and irreversibility

c t       o. 1 or   i .o not see. o    .  .  .bvious counter-

part          atial .rd r.  .e relatio. .e .lves are

ir .        `       .   re .. records t.at c e tri dic r latio.

o. 'bet ... occur. .ot. in the linear spatial series ..d in

tl' te..or 1 series, .t e ph sizes .  a. t .r. is a profound

difference in t c ..ct .enness in eac. c..c.  .e .o.al re-

lation- are analysa le, .ouo .olus, i. ter. s of a sin.le,

asy..etrical dya.ic relation.  In t.c te iporal series there

is an intrinsic .irectio., or  sense". In .e spatial series

there is .c intri..sic .irection; .irectio. can only .e intro-

..cea extri..sically, .it. referenc. to so. e point outside the

series.  In .a.itio., .s .ro.. po.nts ou., s..ce s.. .s to .re-

sup.ose ti e:

     .,atia. extension a.. .ne occ.rre.ce of .patial
relations pr.su. ose te. oral durati n and . certain .e-
ter i ate for. o. ce. poral relation.  .hape a. a size are
co .o ly ascribed to .articulars w ic. persist t .rou.h
perio.s of ti .e ana  ..o .istories o. lon.er or shorter
.uration.  34

    .obb ex.resses t.e differ. .ce bet ecn spatial and ten-

poral rel.tions i. t r s si il r to t ose of .roa., except

that wi.re .roa. co..ic.rs t'e sp tial relation o. 'bet.een"

to be p.rtl. sym. trical nd .rtly a y etrical, .o b o.its

t.is point.

    .ow i. c .si.eri.. t.o subject of time as it
present. .oself to our experience t.ere is one very in-
.ortant respect in v.1c it    ears to .i.fer .ro our
s,.acial exp rie.ce. ..]
    Of a . two instants v ic. one experiences i.
o.e's o.n .ind one is after the other.

> ... is ... a ... it is ... is called an asym-
> metrical relation; ... c i ... ... relation ... .c...
> ... t ... e...'s t relation ... to ... t...en ... oes not bear
> t e rel tion ... to ...
>
> ..., ... particular case consider..., if B is
> ...t r ..., ... ... ... fter ...
>
> ... ...ere however relations w ich are symmetrical;
> such, ... ... ..., ... t c relation of equality, where if
> B is equal to ... n ... is equal to .
>
> ... ... ti ... ... ... ... ...ticles
> in space is a symmetrical relation and, if ... and B be
> ... ...s two ... ... ..., ... ... ... ... re ... ...ly we
> s ould say, t at B is after A ... t...r t... that ... is after ... 35

...ointing ... t that the thought process is essentially
an irreversible one, ...obb goes on to offer an explanation of
the peculiarity of the relations ...ic... gives ther their asym-
metrical c...racte.. ..e fundamental fact, for ...obb, about
these r...tions i... t...at an effect is al...y... after a cause.

> A present action of ti...e may produce so...e effect
> to-morrow, ...t t not i... ...v ich l ...ay do ...ot can have any
> effect on that occurred yesterday. 36

...his ...obb se...s to take the causal relation as the
fundamental one, which enables us to distin tish between
spatial ...d te...poral relations. It may be doubted in passing,
...owever, whether this is entirely defensible since it does
not see... to be the case that all te poral series involve
causation. ...he pain in my toe may be after ry perception of
the flash of li...t, ...t ...oes not see... to h...ve oeen caused
by it. ...he i ...ortant ...oints brou ...t in ...obb's treatment of
temporal re...ations, however, seem to be the same as those
mentioned by broa..., na...ely, the intrinsic successiveness
and irreversibility of the time series. It is these which

in race to suffer from space, or it is damaging to
escape its woe in the or intrinsic analogy between the
realms of time.

In some quarter, however, the arguments of
those who hold that the analogies between space and time do
not break down, and that to a far greater extent than was
formerly realized, what can be said of space can likewise
be said of time, and vice versa. This, we take it, is a
correct statement of the position of those who deny any intrinsic difference between space and time. We shall examine
first some of the arguments presented by Taylor, who gives
a clear statement of his position.

> I want to remove some of this mysteriousness
> (of time) by showing that temporal and spatial re-
> lations, contrary to much traditional thought, are
> radically alike; or, more precisely, that (1) terms
> ordinarily used in a peculiarly temporal sense have
> spatial counterparts and vice versa, and that accor-
> dingly (2) many propositions involving temporal con-
> cepts which seem obviously and necessarily true, are
> just as necessarily but not so obviously true when
> reformulated in terms of spatial relations; or, if
> false in terms of spatial concepts, then false in
> terms of temporal ones too. 37

Taylor has two of his analogies already mentioned,
namely, simple location, and extensive mass involving divisibility into parts. But he also introduces a supposed
analogy in terms of direction, which divides Broad's point
concerning the intrinsic direction or sense of the time-
series.

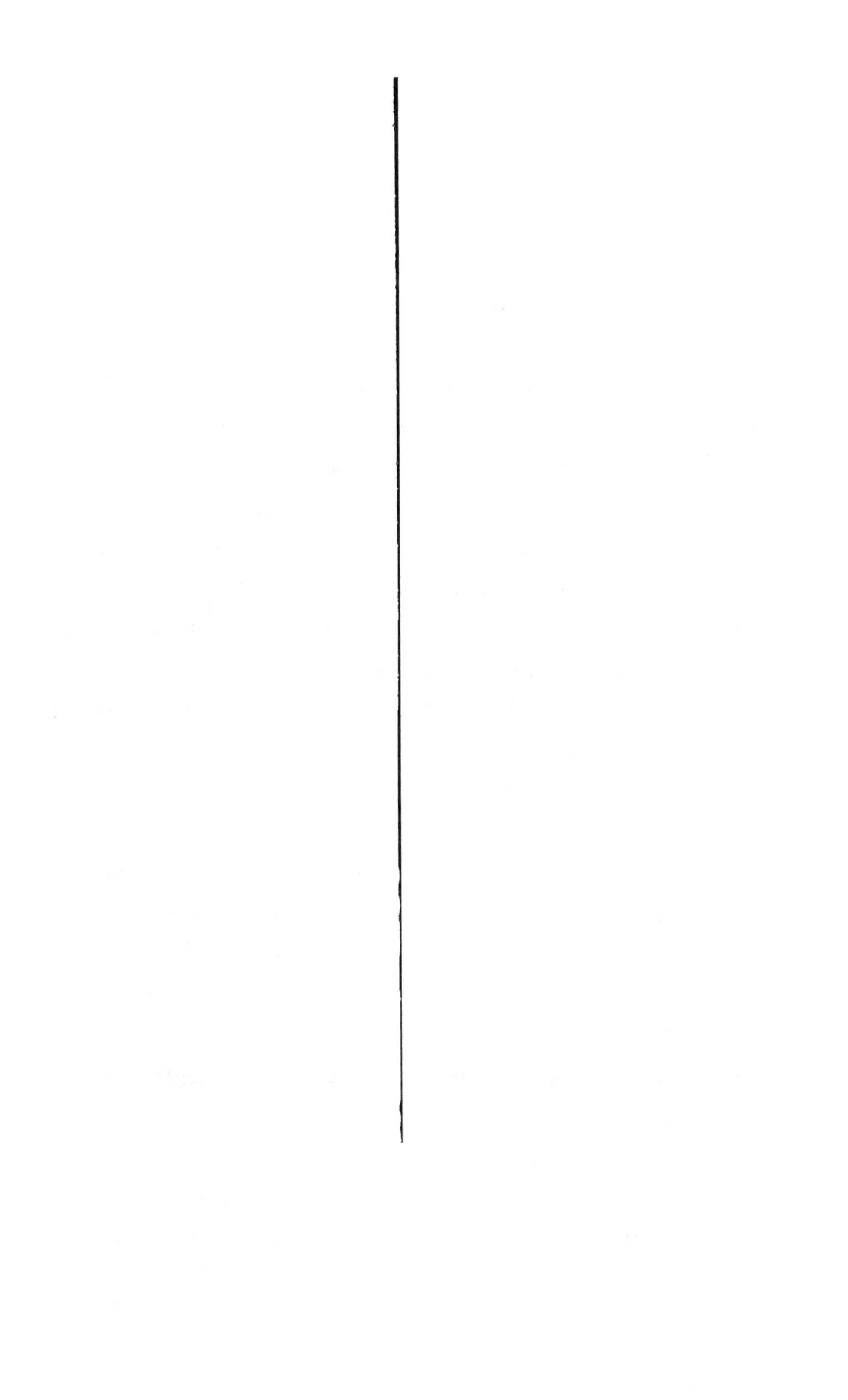

s ct to  ̣ ̣  ̣ i.l  ̣ te  ̣ ̣ I re ti s; one
 ̣ ,  ̣ ̣ ̣  ,  ̣ ̣ ̣  ̣ ̣  r  ̣ ̣ ̣ ro  ̣ ̣ t to
fut're, fro  ̣ t ire to  ast. fr  nort' to sout ̣, a  d
 ̣ ̣ ̣ , n  ̣  ̣ ̣  c  ̣ ̣ ̣ ̣ ̣ ̣   ̣ ̣ ̣ ̣  ;
 ̣n ̣ e or  ̣itriasic t ̣ n t ̣ e  ̣ iors.  3

Taylor  ̣  ̣ s t ̣ is s ̣ te  ̣n ̣  it ̣  ̣ t  ̣ ̣e  ̣ l  ̣
su  ̣o ̣ ̣ it ̣ n a ̣  ̣a ̣ .   ̣ is is  ̣ ̣or ̣ nate  ̣or is c s ̣ ,
since  ̣os ̣ of  ̣is proo ̣s o ̣  ̣ ̣ lo ̣i s  ̣et ̣een s ̣ ce an ̣
time  ̣in ̣ e o ̣  ̣ ̣e tr ̣ t o ̣ i ̣ .  It is o ̣vio ̣ ̣ that if we
deny the essential ch ̣ r c ̣ ristic  ̣hic ̣ ̣istin ̣ uishes space
fro ̣ t ̣ ̣ e, ̣ a nu ̣ ̣er of su ̣ ̣osed analo ̣ ies follow analyti-
cally.  ̣ ̣ s r ̣ ises the interestin ̣  ̣uesti ̣ n of how one
could s ̣o ̣ t ̣ ̣ it th ̣ re are ̣nalo ̣ i s betw ̣en space ̣nd ti ̣ e.
It see ̣ s clear that the fin ̣ l a ̣ eal ̣ ̣st ̣e, broa ̣ ly spea ̣ ing,
to ex ̣ erie ce.  ̣e ̣ c ̣ ̣ not co ̣ c r ̣ o ̣ ̣sel ̣ s ̣ ̣ re ̣ s to
just ̣ ̣at 'ex ̣ eri ̣ ̣ ce" compris ̣ s.   ̣ ̣th ̣ r ̣ ̣ ̣ean "sense-
experi ̣nc ̣ ̣" (s ̣ ̣ in ̣ ,  ̣eari ̣ , f ̣ elin ̣ ,  ̣ stin ̣ , ̣tc.), 'co ̣ ni-
tive ex ̣ erience" (p ̣ rceptual ̣ud ̣ monts, i ̣ tellectual pre-
hensi ̣ n ̣ , ̣tc.), or ex ̣ erience in so ̣ ̣ other  ̣ ̣ in ̣ , ̣s not
so im ̣ ort ̣ ̣ t as t ̣ t ̣ ̣ ̣ ̣ust ̣ ve sc ̣ e ̣ on- r ̣ itrary co ̣ rt
of appeal ̣ ̣ic ̣ ̣ i ̣ l e ̣ able ̣ ̣s ̣o ̣ is ̣ i ̣ ̣ is ̣ bet ̣ een ̣ en ̣ ine
analogy a ̣  ̣ere ̣ ss ̣ pti ̣ n. ̣t is not ̣ ̣ li ̣ ̣ el ̣ , of course,
t ̣ at t ̣ e ̣ ̣ ̣ill be disa ̣ ̣ree ̣ nt concer ̣ ̣ ̣  t ̣ e legiti ̣ acy or
possi ̣ ility o ̣ ̣ x ̣ eri ̣ nc ̣  in its v ̣ rious ̣ ea ̣ in ̣ s. ̣ t it
see ̣ ̣ clear t ̣ at t ̣ e responsibility of tho ̣ e ̣ ̣ ̣ ssert ̣ nalo-
̣ ies between s ̣ ace and ti ̣ e, or ̣nalo ̣ ies i ̣ <u>any</u> context, will
be to indicate what experience of what kind illustrates the

the analogy which they assert.  In the absence of an attempt
to do this, we may feel justified in returning the Scottish
verdict: "Not proven".

No matter what analogous statements we can make concerning space and time, no analogy between space and time
themselves will be demonstrated until it has been shown that
such statements are synonymously true, that is, true in the
same sense.  They need not be entirely synonymous, perhaps,
but they must be synonymous in just those respects which
make them analogous.  That is, it must be shown that the
term "length" or the term "part", for example, has the same
meaning when applied to space and time respectively, and
that true statements can be made involving this meaning in
both contexts.  And this involves, of course, showing that
such terms, if meaningfully applied to space, do in fact
have a meaning when applied to time.  If they have no meaning when applied to time, there can be no synonymy, and
hence no analogy.  But synonymy can only be finally shown
by appealing to experience, in some acceptable sense of the
word.  Thus, for example, we say with perfect candour that
some two-dimensional spaces, i.e. patches, are red, but when
we say that some times are red, the statement seems to be
nonsense.  We have no notion, in terms of our experience,
of what a "red time" as opposed to a "green time" or a
"yellow time", might mean, although we have no trouble in

experience distin_uishin  bet een a red patch and a  rreen or
yellow patch.  Je are not entitl d to a sure synonymy of analogous statements concerning space and ti e, without reference
to our experience of space and time.

Thus, if we say that time has no intrinsic direction,
we must look to our experience to find out whether t is has
a meanin_.  When we do this, it seems that the state ent has
no clear meaning.  For we know what we mean when we say that
an observable spatial series has no intrinsic direction.
Part, at least, of what we mean is that when observing a
series of objects in space, we can, at will, with a flick
of our eyes, run through the series from either end, indif-
ferently, or perform similar operations tactilely.  But if
we are observing a series of events in time, we find that we
cannot, at will, run through the series from either end.
This is not merely a practical difficulty, but is a logical
impossibility, for runnin- through a temporal series from
either end involves holding that a past event can be present
to an observer.  That is, in order for an observer to run
through a temporal series from either end, it is necessary
that events which are past to the observer should be present
to him so that he can run through them in different directions.
But it is a necessary although not sufficient condition for
an event to be past to the observer that it should not be

present to him. He must then observe an event which is both present and not present to him. Whether we consider his observation of this event to be instantaneous or to take an enormous lapse of time is irrelevant. For his act of observation must be considered to be a single act, by which he observes, i.e. has present to him, a single event that is not present to him. We add that a necessary condition of being present to an observer is that the observer should have a sensation, (not necessarily atomic), which is correlated with the functions of his receptors in such a manner that it would not be called a memory.

If it be insisted that the observer's act of observation does take some time during which the same event will be both present and not present (past) to him, and so involves no contradiction, it should be noted that if the event becomes past to him, he is therefore not observing it. Hence his act of observation of the event comes to an end, just when the event becomes past, i.e. not present to him. It will therefore not be correct to say that he observes an event which is both present and not present (past) to him. But the observer must make just such a logically impossible observation in order to run through a temporal series of events from either end.

It is tempting to suppose that the same condition might apply to the observation of a spatial series. This,

however, is not the case, for it is just o c peculiarity of
spatial configurations that they can and often do remain present to an observer during the ti e l e runs through them in
either direction.  In a single act of observation an observer
may run back and forth over a spatial series _that is present
to him during the entire time_.  As in the case of a temporal
series, it is irrelevant how long a single act of observation
may take.  It may be considered to be instantaneous, or to
take an enormous lapse of time.  As a matter of fact the specious present is fairly short, but that has no bearing on the
theoretical aspects of the case.  The specious present may be
as short or as long as we please in terms of units of measured
time; the point is that the whole series of spatial configurations is _present_ to us during the entire time.  If we hold
two fingers in front of our eyes, we can run back and forth
over them in a single act of observation, and while we are
doing so, they are both present to us.  They do not disappear
as a past event disappears. They are definitely not past to
us.  They are present.

It may be objected, however, that we are using the
term "present" in a non-temporal sense, that we are using
it only in the sense of "immediately apprehended", witnessed,
or sensed.  We agree, of course, that when we said that an
object or event was present to an observer, we meant that he
was aware of certain sensations.  But this does not prove that

the usa e is not temporal. It does, ho ever, reveal the difference between ti e as <u>conceived</u> in terms of units of measurement, divisible into parts, and time as it is <u>felt</u>. The object or event which the observer saw was not present to him
in the sense it was an instant or length a certain number of
units removed from some fixed date, it was present to him in
the sense that it was <u>not future</u>, and <u>not past</u>. In other
words, the difference between the observer's apprehension of
the temporal series and his apprehension of the spatial series
is that the former involves a reference to the future and the
past, while the latter does not necessarily do so. The progress of the event from being future to the observer to being
present to him, and to being past to him, is what made him
unable to run through the temporal series from either end.

We therefore maintain that the primary, irreducible,
and intrinsic temporal meaning of the term 'present" is that
of the <u>experience</u> of the present, which involves the distinction between the present which we do experience, and the future and past which we can never experience. If we are to
speak of tire or temporal relations at all, we must be prepared to accept the temporal distinctions which are revealed
in experience, and these, of course, are the distinctions between past, present and future. We have an unmistakable
sense of the difference between the present and the past, and
between the past and the future, and between the present and

both the past an  of  future.  First of all, we are never

in  ou t  s to v iet  or or not we are in the present.  we can

always distin ish the present fro  the f ture and the past.

The future and the  st are, quite simply, not present.  Je

ave an unmistakable sense of the difference between the fu-

ture and the past, how ver, and the clearest proof of this

is that we can remember the past, but not the future.  Russell

says that "it is a  ere accident that we have no memory of

the future".[39]  But an accident due to what?  If we refuse to

accept the fact that we do not have a memory of the future

as _prima facie_ evidence  of the tem oral distinctions between

the past and the future, we shall never oe able to decice the

question of whether the ti e series has an intrinsic direction

or not.  For our awareness of the difference between past,

present and future, as Broad points out, is intimately asso-

ciated with the intrinsic direction or sense of ti e.

> Now the intrinsic sense of a series of events
> in Time is essentially bound up with the distinction
> between past, present, and future.  A precedes B be-
> cause A is past when B is present.  [40]

Furthermore, if the theor  of the four-dimensional

manifold is true, it is not clear how anyone co ld possibly

know that we do not, in fact, have a me ory of the future.

e take for  ranted that memory gives us an awareness of

events which are not present to us.  hether thi  av areness

is "direct" or not, does not matter for the pres nt case,

as lcn  s it is granted that  c ory gives us awareness, in
so e sense, of events which are not present. Let us say,
t'en, th.t the occurrence of a me..ory A '.as a"memory relation
to the occurrence of another event B.  Let .s suppose that A,
is present to sor.e subject who is situated at some specifiable
place in the space-time continuum.  Nor, how this subject
could know that A is related to B in cnc direction of the
time-dimension rather than to ano .er event C in the opposite
direction of the ti e-di.ension, is an interesting question.
.hat possible criteria could he use to decide?  Certainly,
he could n ver decide the question e.pirically, for the positions of '., B, and C are fixed in the space-ti..e continuum,
and neither B nor C are present to the subject.  He could
never compare A with either B or C, as to li'eness.  It is
te.pting to su.pose that at a later specifiable place in the
subject's history, sa:, at the point where  or C occurs, if
his history happens to include either of these points, he
might carry out a co.parison.  But, of cource, A is, a.ain,
not present at B or C, and no empirical check is possible.

It might be objected t.at memory requires repetition,
and that we could easily _define_ a mer.ory as that event which
followed a suitable number of repetitions of a certain experience.  This would not be a valid objection.  First of all,
memory does not always require repetition. Secondly, the
objection does not hold anyway, for obviously we need the

memory relation to relate the memory to the last of the repetitions, w ich by definition is not pres nt to us. We are
still forced to accept a memory which is present to us at
some point of the time-dimension, and which e still do not
know to relate to an event in one direction o the ti e-
dimension or the other. Incidentally, no sort of psychological explanation will answer, for it will presuppose that
memory relates to the past, that is, one te poral direction
rather than another, and further, is likely to involve the
use of memory itself, either in its explaation or in the
empirical investigation on w ich it is based.

It seems evident that if we do not n o the difference
between the future and the past, we can never know to which
of these our memories relate. It is to be noted t at we cannot put this the other way around. Although the distinctions
between past, rresent and future ust be revealed in experience, (otherwise we could never now of them at all), we
cannot _define_ these distinctions i ter s o our cognitive
acts, such as erception and memory. s regards memory, we
cannot define the st as that to which our memories relate,
because we will still not know whether the past is in one
direction of the ti e-di ension or the other. For the same
reason we can ot define the future as that which we do not
or cannot remember, and which is not perceived by us. In
addition, we shall always have difficulty in distinguishin

t' t ' c'   cannot remember bec use it i  fut re fro  t!at
w ic  we do  ot remember bec use our memories are fallible.
 oreover, a  Broa  indicates, every event that an observer
'nows of  ust   ca  ble of bein  both re e bered and perceived.

        'ence these cognitive characteristics do not
suffice to distinguish a past from a present event,
since every event that C knows of has <u>both</u> these relations to him.  If you add that an event always has
the perceptual relation to   efore it has the memory
relation, you only mean that the event of remembering
so ething is present when the event of perceiving it
is past, and you have simply defined present and past
for O's <u>objects</u> in terms of present and past for his
cognitive <u>acts</u>.  If you then try to define the latter
in terms of differ nt relations to C's acts of intro-
spection, you simply start on an infinite regress in
w ic' past and present re ain obstinately undefined
at any place where you choose to stop.  41

These difficulties concerning memory and the attempt
to define the past, present, an  future, are connected with
the view that the analogies between space and time do not
break down.  The supposition that it is a mere accident that
we have no me ory of the future, presupposes that past, present and future do not represent unique temporal dis inctions.
And the view that we can <u>define</u> past, present, and future
likewise assumes that they are not unique distinctions, but
can be understood in terms of somethin  else.  We must now
turn to so e of the specific arguments which Taylor advances
to show that space and ti e are analogous entities.  We shall
not examine all of his argu ents, since most of the  rest on
the same assumptions.  If we can question these assumptions

i.. one case, we can do so in the others.

We have already noted t..at Taylo.. does not _prove_
t..a.. ti..e ..as ..o i..trinsic direction, out assumes it. ..e
also note ..at he likewise do..s not ..rove synonymy of ..he
..erms "place' and 'part" when applied ..o ..pace and time re-
spec..ively. ..it.. these t..in..s in ..ind, we proceed to ex-
a..ine ..i.. first ar..ument. ..aylor's procedure is to state
objections w..ic.. are co....o..ly thou..ht to ex..ress a radical
difference ..etween space and ti..e, and t..en to s..ow that the
objections do not express such a difference. The first objection is as follows:

> ..n o..ject cannot be in t..o places at once, thou..h
it can occupy two or ..ore times at only one place. 42

Taylor ar..ues that since we say that an object is
in one plac.. at two times only if it occu..ies all the time
in between, either at that place or another, we can equally
well say that an object can also be in two places at one
time by occupyin.. the intervenin.. space.

> A ball, for instance, occupies t..o places at
once, if t..e places be chosen as those of opposite
sides; out i..n so doin.., it occu..ies all the places
between. It is temptin.. to say that only _part_ of
the ball is in either place; b..t t..en, it _is_ a different _temporal_ part of a..n object w..ich, at the same
plac.., is in either of two times. 43

..e draw attention, first of all, to the point that
if we do r..ake s..ch statements as that "..n object occupies
all the time in between", we are presupposin.. an analogy
between space and time. If we can make such a statement

with respect to it. In the same sense, (or in any sense),
that we call an... it with respect to space, we grant the whole
analogy, including the curious term 'temporal part". Obvi-
viously if an object occupies time' in the same sense that
it occupies space, we must admit that a identical object
can be extended through one time while its spatial parts
are in different places. This would apply to any object
whatever that we can perceive. The point at issue, however
is just whether we can use such language synonymously with
respect both to space and time, whether, in particular, it
has any meaning to make such statements about time. We m
reiterate here that when we speak of time in this thesis
we are not referring to measured time or physical time, the
concepts of which conform to the requirement of extensiveness, but about time itself. For this reason we have sure
that a theory of time must take account of the way in whi
time is dealt with in various sciences. We cannot assume
uncritically that time is identical with conceptual time.
If we do, we shall be the question of whether or not it
is analogous to space. Time may be a unique entity, incapable of being treated of in terms of concepts such as extensiveness.

The premise of Taylor's argument assumes without
discussion that time and space may be conceived in the sa
terms. It assumes that if we can say that an object occup

space, ..as also cam. fully s.y o ao it 'occupies si.c',
.nd c at  e .ae ao s.y t is, our .tate cne i synony ous
.it .   nalo o s .e to ent conc.rnin. .p ce. ...is, of
course, is j.st t c poi.t at issue as co i nechei chere are
analo.i s ae\.cen s ac  and ti e.  .enco Taylor's ar.u.ents
do not .rove analo ies betwee  sace and ti e.  .hey be; the
 hole questio..

 .aylor's ar.ume t. are b sea on anot. r assumption,
which is relatea to t.e one .e have .entioned. .his concerns
t.c idei tit. of indivi .al t.in...

  For just as we can ardoidinarily do say that
movin· about in space --i.e. acquiring and losin· spatial relati.ns .ith other t.in.s ovei a lapse of time--
does not destroy the identity of a thin·, we have equal
reason to say that .ovin. about in ti.e --i.e. acquirir;
and losin. te.poral relations .itl ot er t.in.s over a
lapse o. space --does not d stroy it eit.er.  44

 .his a su.ftion a ain p. supposes .ath.r than ce on-
strates un analog. betw.en space anc ti e, .nd stan.s or
falls on t e qu stion of w ether t re is s.c. an analogy.
For .e note .hat .aylor co.ceives of the te poral relations
of a t in  in .c ..s of extensiv n.ss.  It is an easy step
to su.pose t.ac a t ing can c'ange its te oral "distance
just as it c.an es ic. s.atial distance .it' respect to
other t.ings, if .e assume in t.e first place that the ter.
"distac.ce" is appropriately us.d of ti.e.  .his furtner step
involves a rep..iation of the point t at .iere is a. intrinsic .irection or sense of the ti.e-series.  For if there

i. no i t. r.ic s .m. .. t. ti.- .'    .c fix s the
t. por l i.l tio. f . .i  .it' os. c. .o o   t i.-s,
w. .y, per   , u., . .l t. r  . . ivid. ls .ic.
c. an . th.ir to oral relatio . .'is .c.. . ril. involves
clan i.. t.. co.ce.ti n of  a. cor. it .  .. .i' .tity of
   thi. .    ca..ot hold .'.t t'.e t.t.. sic 'ea.e of t. e
ti.e-s.ri.s .ixes t'.c t. poral r.latio. . o. .'i.(, without
also holdi., t... t'ere. .re i' .c.. l t i .c to '.. so fixed
in t'eir t '.or.l r.latio... ..t if . .i. t... loc.ri.e,
w. er.se bot. .spects of it.   .c .. ot  .y c.at t'ere is
an intr..sic se... of th. ti. -s.ri. .it.c.t al.o 'e.yi.,
that t.e i.dividu..ls fixe. .. t .. i..r..sic. n.e re i..
dividu..... .or .he i.tri.sic se.s. o'. t'.c ti. -s.ri.s is
expressed .y t'.c .. ct that .. re a. ce..a. identical i..
dividuals, (ot.er. ise ide.tifi.ble t'. ..y ..'.ir te.oral
relations), .ic. .r. fi.c.d a. to t.eir te. oral relations
to other thi... .s, o.. a li.e n..u... It i. o vio.sl. necessary to hold t.at t.ese i.dividu.l.. . ot. . .ise i.enti-
fiable t.an .y their .elations i. t. ti..e-series, for if
their individuality .epe..ded _only_ o. their te oral relations, ther. would be no .eans o.. .ixi., ither their
individuality or .heir te. poral relatio.s. T.is follows
as a direct res.lt of co.c.ivin. t..e a..ter t.e an.lo.y
of . strai..,t li.e. Io. can we i.entify i.dividuals on a
straight line, except by co.vention? But i. the .dividuality

of our time-span, and ... is ... so is a line, or in
time, (conceived in this manner), is ... or fixed by some
other means, the ... spatial ... be go ... relations in
of ... two classes, respectively, re ... to a line. ... as the
... or, relations that time is ... series ... is an intrinsic sense, ... also hold that the individuality of the
events in ... series is constitutive of the temporal relations. Individual events, so to speak, ... l'or their way
into their positions in the time-series.

It must be admitted of this theory ... it conceives
of the time-series with an intrinsic ... direction, 'the sort
of thing we usually represent by a straight line with an
45
arrow-head on it, is rather unsatisfactory. It seems to
be a sort of half-way house on the road to a theory of
the space-time manifold. This is not to say, however, that
there is not an important element of truth in the view that
time has an intrinsic direction or sense. Whether this point
is adequately or falsely expressed in terms of a series with
a direction, however, is a matter we shall discuss further
on. For the present, it remains to compare the merits of
this theory which does maintain a fundamental distinction
between space and time, with the theory which denies this
distinction.

We have already drawn attention to the point that
there is a close connection between the view that the

ti e-se ies  ..  n intrinsic sense,  nd   e i cntit; of individuals.  I e d ial of t is positi n involves holdin~
that not only is extensiveness and its r_lated properties,
attributa le both to space and tine, but also that time
in no way has an intrinsic direction w ich space has not.
.e have noted that Taylor h s not proved a) analo7y in this
respect, but  as assumed it.   e enqire no w ether an,one
could possibly prove it.  If we find reaoon to believe that
it is impossible to prove this  alogy, and ve find ood
reasons for not accepting it, ve shall, by this token, have
good re~sons for rejecting the theory of the space-ti e manifold.

It is to be observe that  enying t'at the ti e-series
has an intrinsic dir ction involves holdia  that i dividuals
are not in any sense given.   corollar, of this is the vie.
that it is a atter of choice or convention as to what we
consider to be an i dividual.  For if  hold that individuals are i any ense iven to us in experience, or fixed
other ise tha by convetion, and if e hold likeviso that
time is ad.qi tely conc ived i ter s of extensiven s,  e
ust a mit that the occure ce of t se i dividuals unalter-
ably fixes t'ir te oral relations i ti.e.  If we vant to
old that te oral rel tions of t'i s ca. chaie, e rust
abandon the notici t t indivi'uals re i any sease ivon,
or fixed otherwise than by convention.  It is to be noted

i[illegible] i r xt ve-
, i [illegible]d. [illegible]oi [illegible] exte sive ess
[illegible]lf, ___ [illegible], o. c. l [illegible] r i [illegible]
a cc [illegible]o. [illegible]ividu [illegible]. [illegible] [illegible]. or t is is t[illegible] t
[illegible] [illegible] c [illegible] [illegible] lo.o [illegible] o [illegible], ev [illegible] [illegible]ere lit rally
t [illegible]. [illegible] i [illegible]v [illegible]s [illegible] to [illegible] i it, t eir idi-
vidu[illegible]i [illegible] cc fr s [illegible] [illegible] else. [illegible]sivcness
[illegible]i [illegible] o [illegible] o [illegible], i div uals [illegible] [illegible] l [illegible] in it onl[illegible]
by co v [illegible] [illegible]. [illegible]xt [illegible] [illegible]s [illegible] l t i divi u ls, [illegible]ut
i [illegible] [illegible]ct [illegible]cc [illegible] for, or be c [illegible] itutive of _diff re t_ indivi u ls. [illegible] [illegible]v ry [illegible]ere t [illegible]sa [illegible], t [illegible] re [illegible]o differentiation [illegible] i [illegible], [illegible]nc [illegible]o [illegible]if[illegible]ren [illegible] [illegible]vidu l , exce t
[illegible] [illegible] f [illegible] [illegible] [illegible] are choro [illegible] i[illegible] [illegible]ifi [illegible] so t in
o tsi [illegible]. [illegible] [illegible] [illegible]io [illegible] o [illegible]or, [illegible] [illegible] i[illegible] if, in-
dividu ls [illegible] [illegible] [illegible] [illegible]t li [illegible], [illegible]cupt b [illegible] c [illegible] [illegible]ic [illegible] ence,
t [illegible] [illegible]o [illegible]ol[illegible] t e t[illegible]cory of [illegible] [illegible]ac[illegible]ti c [illegible]ifold, o an
e t nsive c [illegible] l [illegible], ar [illegible]al [illegible] lo ical [illegible] [illegible], if t e[illegible] hold
t [illegible]t i [illegible]iv [illegible]uals [illegible] i [illegible] [illegible]ifi ble onl [illegible] [illegible] c [illegible] [illegible] tio . It
is [illegible] lo ic l s [illegible], [illegible]c use [illegible] i [illegible]ivi ul ty o [illegible] [illegible]ivi u ls
must pro [illegible]d fr [illegible] [illegible] et i [illegible]o usi [illegible] t e [illegible]xt [illegible]sive conti um
i self. [illegible] [illegible]t i [illegible] d [illegible] [illegible] le te , o ever, is ano-
t er questio [illegible], [illegible] i [illegible] thi [illegible] r [illegible] r [illegible] o e [illegible] [illegible]t ell as [illegible] o
a yon [illegible] co ld __c [illegible] [illegible]t so [illegible] i [illegible] [illegible]s a [illegible]t er cf co v tion.
It [illegible]ight [illegible]e [illegible] [illegible] s ell [illegible]het [illegible]r c [illegible]v [illegible]ti [illegible] lity its lf
i [illegible] [illegible]tt r o [illegible] c v ti [illegible], [illegible] [illegible] discu [illegible]io of t [illegible]is o ll

make us too far afield.

One of the primary reasons for him for rejecting the theory of the four-dimensional manifold, in which time is conceived as a fourth dimension, is that it does not seem to be the case that all events are capable of being located in such an extensive continuum. Some events, e.g. feelings and thoughts, seem to take place in time alone. Yet, if the four-dimensional manifold contains all events, all events must *ipso facto* be capable of being located by three spatial coordinates and one temporal one.

In addition, if it is held that there is no distinction between space and time, and that time has no intrinsic *sense*, this will mean, as we have already mentioned, that individuals will be a matter of convention. If this is explicitly maintained, as Taylor and Williams do, it must also be admitted that it would be fruitless to refer to experience in order to determine whether time has an intrinsic direction or not. Hence we could never decide this question one way or the other, with respect to our experience of space and time, for it would depend on our choice of individuals. We could choose individuals which move either back or forth in time, or both, as Taylor, in fact, does.[46] This is a direct result of supposing that an individual can change its temporal relations without losing its identity. From the standpoint of our experience of space and time, this

[illegible] [...] rd [...] [...] [...]
in " [...] iv [...] do [...] [...] i [...] relation-[47]
[...] [...] 'o t' ir [...] l cal t' [...]ips",
ives [...] [...] utr [...] [...] vie [...] t' t individual [...] c' n [...] 'eir temporal r[...].

> "[...] to opinion [...] verbal acci-
> dent. Why not simply generalize the use of "change"
> [...] lit'l [...] so [...] thin ch[...]es in [...] iven respect
> if different parts of the thing have different quali-
> ti s of t [...] kind i[...] pe[...]io[...]. [...]eca se, it [...] be
> fairly answered, this ignores the distinction between [...]
> a [...] [...] [...] [...] 'i [...] t'[...] t travels [...]ve[...] [...]ive[...] region,
> and a spatially large thing that occupies a comparable
> region a[...] sir le inst rt. [...]c[...] c[...] the two t'ings
> has parts that differ fro[...] one anot[...]er in location;
> b[...]t [...]ccor[...] to or[...]inary us[...]e, only the former un-
> der [...]o[...] chan[...]e. By applyin[...] th[...] term "change" in the
> one c[...], [...]t ot t'e t'er, or i[...]ar[...] [...]re marks an
> important distinction. 48

For reasons suc' as there, I reject the theory of

the four-dimensional manifold in which all events are lo-

cated, and we retain the view that there is a fundamental

distinction between space and time. To the examination of

the nature of t[...]s distinctior, we [...]st now proceed.

CHAPTER IV

QUALITATIVE CONCLUSIONS AND THE FLOW

OF TIME CONCE...

3.  <u>The Direction of Time and the Problem of Individuation</u>

First of all, we will enquire how it is that time
or the time-series, conceived as a unidimensional extensive
continuum, gets its intrinsic direction.   We have already
pointed out that it involves a logical contradiction to sup-
ose that we can run through a temporal series from either
end.   We should have to observe at least one event that was
both present and not present (past).   This consequence
follows from the primary temporal meaning of the term "present,"
namely, the "present" of a conscious observer.   If we regard the term "present" simply as a synonym for "being at"
some point in the time continuum, of course, such a present will be both present, and past with reference to some
other point on the continuum.   But such a use of the term
"present" will not give us any intrinsic direction of
the time-series, for we could equally well refer to the
past in either direction.   We should not know whether our
memories referred to events in one direction of the time-
series or another, and this difficulty would  present

65

itself for every year a memory then and d.  These
are some of the points rel tin  to  intrinsic direction of the time-series,  ich e  ve  ac in th
course of our ar um nt.  Finally, we main ain d th t huma
bein s have an unmistakable awareness of the distinction
between past, resent, ni future.  It remains now to
try to show whence the e distinctions arise, and hence
how it comes to be hel  th t th re is a time-series which
has an intrinsic sense or direction.

It is to be emphasized that this conception of
time, conceives it as a _series_.  How, then, we ask, does
_any_ series get  direction?  It is a  rent tl t no
series can get a direction if it i  iven whole.  It will
as Broad says, have an _order_ but not a direction.

> The peculiarity of a series of events in Time
> is that it has not only an intrinsic _order_ but also
> an intrinsic _sense_.  Three points on   tr i ht line
> have an intrinsic order, i.e. B is between A and C,
> or C is between B and  , or  is between C  u  .
> This order is independent of any tacit ref rence to
> something traversin  the line in a certain direction.

It is clear that if time is conceived as _only_
a line, or _series_, in a one-dimensional continuum,  iven
whole, as a series, it simply will not h ve any intrinsic
direction at all.  One c n run t  ou h any serie: _qua_
series, in either direction provided it is suitably
finite.  Somethin  ore ne s to be a ded to it, in order

to give the intrinsic direction. The first thought
that occurs, as Broad hints above, is that of something
traversing the series in a fixed direction. We have ourselves made use of this device in speaking of "running
through" a series from either end. It is a clear enough
means of expressing the idea of direction, but is it
defensible to use it with respect to the time-series?
Can we think of time as a series of events along which
something moves? Broad has expressed this possibility
in a picturesque manner.

> We are naturally tempted to regard the
> history of the world as existing eternally in a cer-
> tain order of events. Along this, and in a fixed
> direction, we imagine the characteristic of pre-
> sentness as moving, somewhat like the spot of light
> from a policemen's bull's-eye traversing the fronts
> of the houses in a street.          50

The difficulties with this, however, are all
too evident, as Broad, himself, emphasizes. Williams
brings them out sharply with one pointed remark: "The
bubble is pricked at once by the question, 'How fast does
the bull's-eye move'?"[51] The answer is, of course, that
it can have no velocity at all, since average velocity
is expressed as the ratio of distance travelled over
length of time. But the bull's-eye does not move
spatially. It moves supposedly through time. How can
something move without velocity? If the bull's-eye is

conceived to be the specious present of a conscious being, as the analogy suggests, the situation is no different. In the process of pointing out why we cling to an analogy between space and time after it breaks down, Goodman finds the following mistake:

> In the third place, I think our error is nourished by a nebulous underlying notion of the self as something that flits through time carrying its specious present along with it. I have no idea of discussing the nature of the self here; but whether it is or is like a thing, event, or quality-- or whatever else it may be or may be like-- and however many are the times it lights upon, the statement that it lights upon or occupies or is at _different times_ at _different times_ will still be absurd. 52

It is apparent, then, that the notion of a moving self or _anything_ moving along the time-series itself, cannot account for the intrinsic direction of the time-series. What remains to account for it? The answer can only be, we believe, that when time is conceived as a series of events in one dimension stretching into the past, it is also conceived of as _having one end open_ in the specious present of a self. At this open end of the series, events occurring in the specious present are added to the series. The continuous adding on of events at one end of the series gives it an intrinsic sense. The series goes in a fixed direction because it is continuously projecting at the open end. This coincides with

## 69

Kin 's view.  Speakin  of the pr        al  ay c  n i  ,

Kin    oes on to say th-t:

>          e have no ri ht to assume th  t the Present,
> as the locus of motion and becomin , roceeds throu h
> a series of instants like that found in the slices
> of that which has become, and upon which  e have b sed
> our theory of chan e.  Such an assum tion results,
> as we shall atte pt to show, in the  ostulation of an
> absolute s ace and time within which nature works.
> And the failure to  uard a ainst this commonsense
> assum tion ends inevitably in the spatial analogy
> fallacy.       53

This position entails the view that the future does not exist.  Both Broad and King accept thi  result. But as  illiams objects, arguments to  rove the non-entity of the future could equally well  e used to  rove the non-existence of the past, the existence of which both Kin  and Broad uphold, since the past is in the category of that which <u>has become</u>.  If this were a valid objection, it would be fatal to Broad's and Kin 's conception of time as a series of events which have become, stretching into the past, and o en at one end. Clearly, time cannot be a series of events, if these events do not exist.  There is the furth r difficulty, analogous to that of the movin  bull's-eye of the present, namely, the  uestion: "How fast does the becomin  or chan e proceed?"  Kin  answers this objection by declaring that "it is meaningless to say that the Present,

the locus of the act of becoming, is either durative or instantaneous, terms which have reference only to physical time and its divisions".[54]

Although we disagree with the theory we are now discussing on essential points, we believe that Kin 's reply to the above question is essentially the correct one, and that it represents an insight which will lead to the unravelling of some of the mysteries associated with time, space and change. We turn, therefore, to the analysis of the relationships between these three.

To begin, we reaffirm a point which we have already emphasized, namely, that if either space or time or both are conceived as homogeneous, extensive continua, the individuals which appear in such homogeneous media must get their individuality from some source or principle outside the continua. For a homogeneous continuum is literally, everywhere the same. It is to be noted that when space and time are considered to be extensive, they are also conceived to be homogeneous, infinitely divisible and continuous. If we do not hold that individuals are a matter to be decided by convention, and we conceive of space and time in this manner, we must admit that once the individuals are given to these media respectively, the spatial and temporal relations of

them are forev r fixed.  This does not, of course, mean
that the in ividu ls coul  not "move", or th t from the
point of view of our conce tions of  otion, we should be
presented with a static, "block universe".  Individuals
mi ht move, i.e. chan e their extensive rel tionships,
either spatially or temporally, depending on the kinc of
individuals that were  iven.  If we conceive of space and
time as extensive, the only rational way in which to regard
motion is to look upon it simply as the fact that an
individual _is_ _at_ different places  t di fferent times.  As
Russell says:

> It was only recently th  it became possible
> to explain motion in detail in accordance  ith Zeno's
> platitude, and in opposition to the  hilosopher's
> paradox.   e may now at last indul e the comfortable
> belief that a body in motion is just as truly where
> it is as a body at rest.  Motion consists merely in
> the f ct that bodies are sometimes in one  lace and
> sometimes in another, and that they  re at intermediate
> places at intermediate times.     55

There is, however, a difficulty in this doctrine
of motion.  The difficulty is not merely the seeming un-
believableness of the doctrine, from the point of view of
our psycholo ical experience of motion, but rather th t
the doctrine is e istemologically inadequate.  For motion,
we sup ose, always has some direction.  If we rega d
_motion_ as _solely_ a matter of an individual  ein  t
different  laces at di f rent times, we shall be hard

pressed to say in what direction the individual moves.
Direction has simply been left out, except where it is
tacitly retained in the notion of an intrinsic direction
of the time series, so that it is assumed that when an
individual is at different places at different times, the
times are in a linear series from earlier to later.  This
involves, as we have seen, the view that there are
individual events the position of which is fixed in the
time-series which has one open end constantly being pro-
jected.

 We see, then, that there is a mutual relation between the existence of individuals and their extensive
relations in space and time.  How are these individuals
to be distinguished in the homogeneous extensive continua
of space and time?  The answer must be that changes or
differentiations of something extended in space or time,
must be given.  These individual changes or differences
of the extended in space or time must be the distinguishable
individuals in these continua.  But if these were the only
kind of individuals, we would not be able to say that
anything _moved_, either in space or in time.  Movement con-
sisting, as we have seen, according to this way of regarding space and time, of the fact that something _is at_

v rious  l ces,  all  c  th  e i  ivi 'ual  di f  ences  u in
just  i  e   i 'f  nces in  the continuu , ill o  them will
. here th y 're  n  ill not  ove.   .  ere that we
are not speakin  of the  henomenon of motion, but of
motion of an individual considered abstr ctly in the continuum of either s ace or time.  Such "motion" will be
equivalent to the locus of a po nt as tre ed in mathematics.  The point does  ot move in the  henomenal
sense, but is at various points cap ble of  ein  loca ed
by means of distances from fixed coordinates.

Clearly, the di ferences in the extensive continua of space  nd time coul  no  be considered, by themselves, to  e in ividuals in motion, althou h they are
individual  i ferences.  The e must be somethin  in
addition to these, or un erlyin  them, the conce tual
function of which is to constitute the i entity of an
individual in these di ferences, or, through chan es.
The somethin  which answers to these  equir ents is,
of course, the concept of substance.   e hasten to  dd
that we wish to  e un erstood to me n no  ore here than
the principle which accounts for unity o  continued
identity of an in ividual in various differentiations
of the continua.  For our purposes, we  ish to i nore
other possible connotations of the term "substance",

an consider only its function a a principle of individuation.

Traditionally, the substance which has been thought
to have an intimate relation to time, rather than to space
an the material world, is variously designated as _mind_,
_spirit_, _intellect_, _consciousness_, _self_, the _subject_,
the _soul_. These terms, whatever else they may convey,
all carry the connotation of something which retains its
identity in different states in time, or, in our sense,
_moves_ through temporal differentiations without losing
its identity. On the other hand, the substance which is
thought to retain its identity in different parts of space,
or move through space, is _matter_, _body_ or material substance. Hence spiritual substance is the principle of
individuation of something which moves in time, and
material substance is the principle of individuation of
something which moves in space. And in both cases, it is
simply a matter of being, in some sense, _in_ various
differentiations in the extensive continua of space and
time.

This dualism of space and time, corresponding to
the dualism of matter and spirit, however, gives rise to
certain problems. There is apt to be confusion in distinguishing the roles of the two substances, and stating

t . l tion, ay, u n e  vo a  a-
li  ely  r wn th distinction as sh rply s o ible
in o der to cl rify th  1 su  invol ed.  t it  clo r
that th  i tinction i  unsatisfactory from the point of
vi w of ex lainin  h  n ex rience, whicl, .  we mention d e rlier  em  to invol  a s  io-tem or l urity.
 e may ' onder, for exa  le, wheth r two substances re
necessary, or vhether one woul  b  adequate to  ccount
for  ll as ects of human experience.  So f r, we h ve
s oken as if the s atial differences and the tem oral
diff rences were ent rely distinct.  This o viously needs
to be modified if the du lism is to be removed   If we
sup ose th t we need only one subs nce, it will be necessary not only to  eject the  edundant substance, out
also to brin  those di ferentiation  nativ  to the rejected substance into rel tion  ith the  cce ted substance and its differentiations in its pa ticular continuum.  This will involve two points: (a)  e must literally i entify the differenti tions native to the rejected substance with eith r all or some of the differentiations in th  continuum throu h  hich the acce ted substance moves, and (b) we must try to  how th t laws  r
princi les  hich  ov rn the  o  nents or activities of
the accepted subst nce in its own continuum  lso  ov rn

to differentiation in one of the continuum. Thinking
along these lines, one will be led to choose one of two
possibilities which then follows.

(1) There is a principle of individuation
(substance) for space, and this accounts for the events
in the time continuum.

(2) There is a principle of individuation for time,
and this accounts for the objects in space.

Insofar as metaphysics takes space and time to be
extensive continua, these are, we take it, two basic
metaphysical positions.  In both, the conceived substance
will do double duty in the two continua, or either will
have one function for those differentiations which are
common to both space and time.  But it is possible, of
course, that either of these positions may be maintained
with respect to space and time without an attempt being
made to carry through the requirements of a complete
metaphysical system.

Possibility (A), therefore, may be part of a
full-blown materialistic system like that of Hobbes, or
it may be presented simply as a theory concerning space
and time.  It is in latter guise that we meet with it
in classical physics, and in the views of Broad and others.

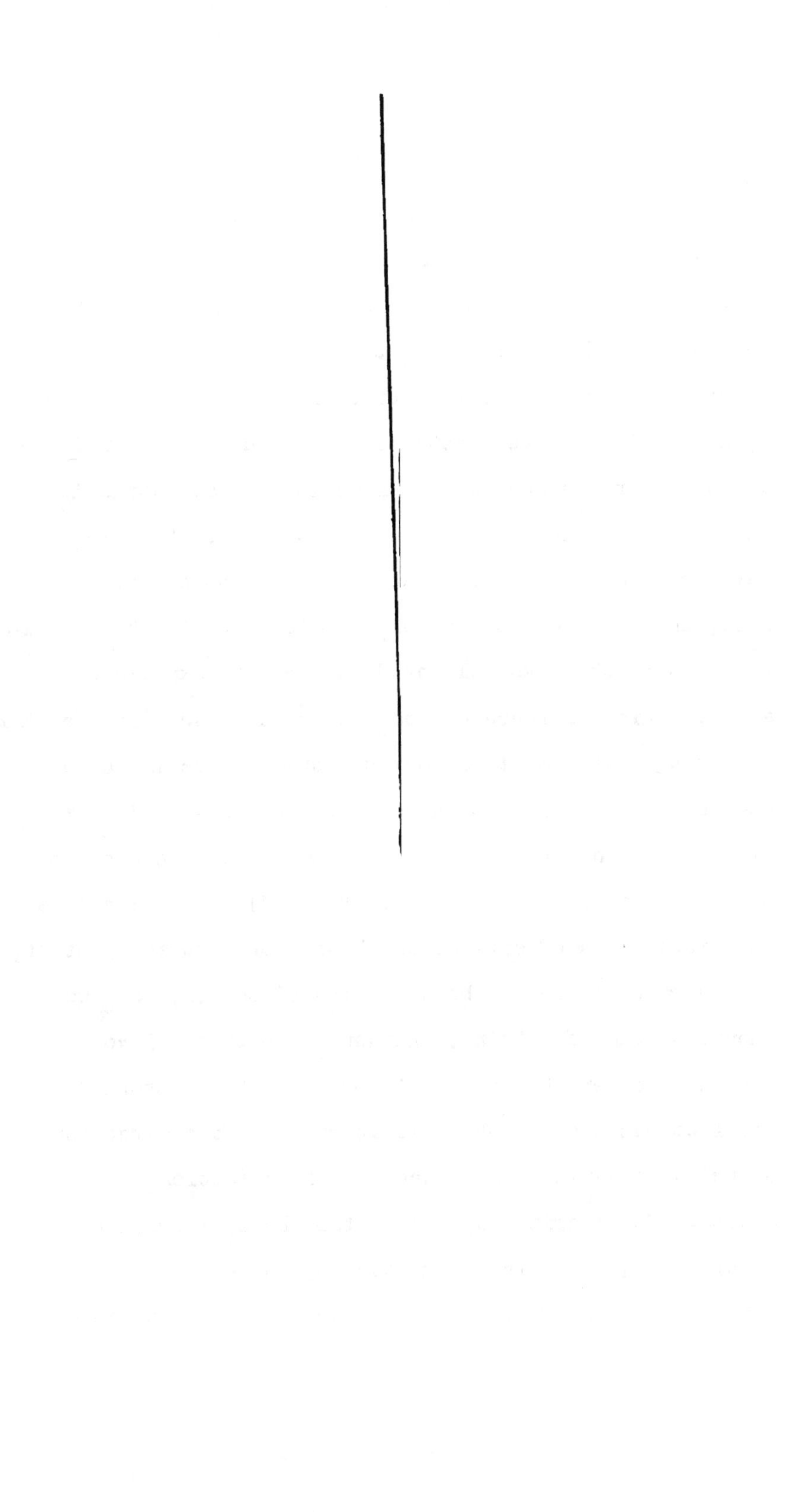

## 77

It allows us to make a fundamental distinctio                    n
space and time, because the ... in ... h spatial relations of objects are thought to be events in time.
Provided it is thought that time is a series with one end
open and with events constantly being added, time will be
different from space in that it will have an intrinsic
sense or direction.  It is to be noted that this view
involves a necessary reference to consciousness or the
self, in order to account for the direction in which motion
proceeds in the physical world, as we have explained
above.  This reference can be expressed in two ways, either
by saying that time is a series with a projecting open
end, or by referring to the observation of the direction
of motion by an observer.  Since the latter, (except for
special cases in the "specious present") always involves
the distinction of earlier and later, or past and present,
in the recognition of the direction of motion, the two
amount to the same thing.  Although the physical world
accounts for events in the time-series, the temporal
distinctions made by the self account for the direction
of the time-series, and hence for the direction of all
motion.  Considering objects in the physical world to
be simply individuals or substances, which are at
different places, neither the direction of the time-series,

nor the direction of any motion would be possible without
this irreducible reference to the observer or the self.
In empirical science, of course, this reference is taken
for granted as generalizations concerning events in the
physical world are only possible where empirical observations are possible.

It is clear that according to possibility A,
when reference is made to the temporal distinctions of
the self, that spatial relations of objects may change
but temporal relations of events may not.[56] Thus, spatial
relations of individual objects may change, and these
changes are considered to be events which take their place
on the end of the time-series. This involves saying that
the object or substance endures through changes in its
states or spatial relations. Since the object retains
its identity through changes in its spatial relations,
and since these changes mark "events" which are fixed
in the time-series, we say that an objects <u>endures</u>,
or is permanent, through time. Here we note the first
requirement of the theory being presented, that is, the
literal identification of changes or differentiations
in the spatial continuum with differentiations in the
time-continuum. Thus differentiations in the time-
continuum are considered to be individuals, and these

get their identity fro  the changes in the sptial relations of objects.  But, as we pointed out earlier, where
differentiations in an extensive continuum are considered themselves to be individuals, they cannot <u>move</u>.
They are irrevocably fixed.  The kind of individual
which is thought to move through time, namely, the self,
has been rejected and the differential individuals must
remain in the position in which they occur in the time-
continuum.  There is, however, the other requirement of
a complete metaphysic, **viz**., that all events in the time-
continuum must be subject to the laws which govern the
activities of the substance which moves through space.
This involves accounting for all those phenomena for
which the rejected substance might have been thought
to account.  Since the spiritual substance which moves
through time has been rejected, it is necessary to show
that all those different states through which the spiritual substance is thought to retain its identity at
different times, are, in fact, subject to the laws which
govern the activities of material substance.  This is a
corollary of maintaining that all events in the time-
continuum are quite literally changes in the spatial
continuum. This necessitates an atte pt to formulate a
materialistic psychology.[57]

metaphysical systems stem in from possibilities
A and B, both invol e hol in  that there is <u>on  n  ure</u>,
the differentiations of which constitute di ferentiations
in th  extensive continuum of both space and tir e.  There
is this di ference between them, ho ever, that while the
materialistic system must deny that there are differ ntia
which appear in the time-continuum alone, for examp.e,
states of mind which are in time, but are non-spatial,
the system which acce ts the self as its sole substance
may maintain that there are differentiations which are
in time alone, without abandonin  the idea th t there
is one nature.  It will only be neces ary to maintain
that all spatial differentiations a e in time, while time
may contain differentiations which are not in space.
This, as we shall see, is the position adop ed by Kant.
The corollary of this latter position i  that it will
be necessary to show that those differentiations which
are in the spatial continuum are subject to those
princi les which govern the activities of the self.
We add that there is, of course, a wide latitude of
possible opinion as to what these activities peculiar
to the self are.  The self may be conceived  s a set
of purely lo ical functions or it may be conceived as a
centre of feelin  and prehensions.  In addition, the

self or subj ct  hich  unctions    rinci le of in-
ivi u tion may  e consi ered monistically or  lural-
istic lly.  N ture may  e the resul  of activities of one
subject or   plur lity of them.

For eit  r theory, the  a    ch n es of the extended are considered to be in  oth sp ce and time.  If
this ste  w re not taken, th re wo l  be no ex lainin
a unity of n ture.  Accordin  to  ossibility (A) chan es
of objects a e considered to be events which  re added
to the end of t   time-series.  Future tim  oes not
exist.  Accordin  to  o sibility ( ), th re  re events
which occur on the en  of the time-series,  nd these
events brin  objects in space into existence.  Time is
the becomin  or   ssin  away of objec s in space.  In
both cases, the sa e, often en irically observ le,
chan es a  e dealt with.  Thus, the main difference between the two theories is a diff rence of e  hasis, and
a di ference of opinion as to what the substance or
principle of in ividuation relates to.  Accordin  to
( ), substance relates to bo ies, o j cts in space,  nd
the chan es throu h which substance r  ains its identity
are thou ht to  e ev nts in time.  Accor din ly, time is
merely a device for recordin  the ch n es of o jects.
It is _deriv tive_, and since it cannot be per ceived, is

sometimes thought to be unreal.  Although it is necessary,
on this theory, to refer to the temporal distinction
of the observer in order to account for the direction of
motions, it need not be considered that anything arises
or passes away so far as the representation of motion is
concerned.  Motion need be considered as nothing more
than the order of the existence of parts of an object.
As to how it comes about that an object is at different
places at different times, this theory need not be concerned.

But according to (B), the principle of individuation relates directly to change itself, to the
successive advance of time.  <u>Objects</u> are derivative.
The self remains the same.  According to (A), space
exists as a whole, and the principles which govern the
movements of bodies may be thought to <u>determine</u> what
changes shall occur in the spatial continuum, and hence
also what events shall appear in time.  According to
(B), space does not exist in itself, as a void awaiting
changes in it, but space as extensive is only an abstract aspect of the primordial becoming of things. The
changes which bring objects into existence also bring extended space into being.  There is just so much space as
the changes of time determine that there shall be.  (A)

consi.. s t.   .  c    .  c  j.c     lo ic lly
prior to ti.  .. c . n e.  (B) consi ... c' .   to be
lo ically prio. to sp c.. . its o'jects.

There is a. t to b. confusion a. to t. term
"time", which h . di ferent m .nin s .cco 'in  to each
theory.  For (A), ti le is mea ured time, ultimately derived from the re_ularity of .vents, .hich .., in turn,
dependent on the .ovement of bo'ies in s.ace.  For (.),
time is a successive series of .cts of .eco in  itself.
Lo ically conceived, time is .or .oth theories a continuum m de u. of .oints .hich .re events or chan.es.
But (A) disre.ards the f ct that the continuum i. ade
up o. ch n es .nd con.i..rs only its lo.ic.l as.ect as
a continuu..  T.c result of this is .. .t tL.e is conceived a. . kind of extensiveness.  In conceivin. of time
in this manner, theory (A) .oints in th. dir.ction of
the theory of the four-.imensional ..nifol. in .hich
there is no necess..ry distinction bet. .en space and time.
It is thus  s .e h ve said . h.l.-.ay house  osition,
which only m.na .es to make . .istinction .. een o. ce
and time by su..o.in. that the time-series is .rojectin.
itself .. one end in the for. o. ne. .vents.  Strictly
s.eakin. , i. i. im.ossible to conceive ho. time, on this
view, coul. project itself.  For the instants of time are

analogous to point on a line, and no matter what point
we take, there is no next point, just as there is no
fraction which is next after it. But it is necessary that
the time-series should project itself, or it would have
no intrinsic direction. If this intrinsic direction is
given up, there will be no distinction between space and
time, and theory (A) will have developed into the theory
of the manifold, the difficulties of which we have already
examined.

Theory (B), on the other hand, does not lose
sight of the fact that time is conceived as a series of
changes. It is possibly for this reason that time has
often been said to flow. We date changes, not objects,
and time is conceived as an extensive continuum of changes.
The thought may arise that the whole continuum is changing
from point to point. Time flows. But this is a mistake,
because even though the continuum is a series of changes,
it does not itself change. The mistake is encouraged,
perhaps, by the fact that in terms of measured time
phenomenal changes take some time to occur.

Nevertheless, the emphasis which theory (B)
places on the fact of change is not lightly to be cast
aside. We have seen that the temporal distinctions of
the self, which are related to the apprehension of change,

.e necessary i o  o ccoun or  l ction of
otion. Theory ( ) oints tow ds  coi l  jection
of  or l istinctions known to the elf, ( ith dis-
stro s results). Theory ( ) ta es these  oral distinction  erio sly and  eant to co bin subject
of c n e with n e teisiv theory of time. For this
re son it considers c ne to  lo ic lly  rior to objects and  ace, nd its rinci le rel tin to th unity
of  ure are principl s which a ly directly to time
itself. Th  rinciples are t en to be as oci ted  ith
the elf o  bjec , which ret ins its i entity through
chan e of time, o  trou  the process of becomin and
assin  ay of objects. Theory ( 3) tt pts to t ke
advanta e of the close connection etween the self-
identity of th  subject and clan , so th t activities
of the self are thought to det r ine the occurrence of
ev nts and hence the co an  to bein  of obj cts. But
it leads lo ically to  jection of ny conce t of the
extensiveness of time. It leads to the fullest acceptance
of the s bjective a rehension of beco in .

 e have h re inten ed to re ent in  eneral the
outlines of these two possibilities before turning to a
specific examin tion of Kant's vie s.  e ho e to show
th t K nt's theory of s ce nd ti e a roxim tes to

ossibility ( ) or other than ( ).   But determining

objects to possibilities, however, to clarify ant's

method of distinguishing between space and time, and his

distinction between inner and outer sense.  To this task

we may proceed.

The doctrine that concepts, (intellectual functions) can only yield knowledge when related to intuitions given to sensibility may be regarded as a view
typical of Kant's mature critical philosophy.  It is a
view which Kant had not clearly arrived at in the
<u>Inaugural Dissertation</u>, indeed, since he does not seem
then to have separated so clearly and sharply the intuitive elements in knowledge from the intellectual.
Yet the trend towards the critical philosophy is quite
evident.  While it is not the purpose of this thesis to
trace the development of Kant's views which culminated
in the position adopted in the <u>Critique of Pure Reason</u>,
a short excursus into the difference between his distinction between space and time in that work, and the
distinction put forth in the <u>Inaugural Dissertation</u>
may serve to throw the doctrines of the <u>Critique</u> into

in the <u>Inaugural Dissertation</u> as sharply as he did in the
<u>Critique</u>.  Similarly, the position adopted in the former
work on the question of the intellect's relation to time
was expressly repudiated in the latter work.

In the <u>Critique</u> the highest principle of all
analytic judgments is held to be the principle of contradiction, a purely negative criterion of truth, necessary but not sufficient to guarantee the correct-
ness of all judgments.

> The principle of contradiction must there-
> fore be recognized as being the universal and complete
> sufficient principle of all analytic knowledge; but
> beyond the sphere of analytic knowledge, it has, as
> a <u>sufficient</u> criterion of truth, no authority and
> no field of application.      58

The principle of contradiction, as characteristic
of the logical functions of the intellect is not, indeed,
ignored or omitted in the <u>Inaugural Dissertation</u>.  There,
instead of making the critical distinction between analytic and synthetic <u>judgments</u>, the use of the intellect
is likewise two-fold, but is on the one hand <u>real</u>, in
which "the very concepts of objects or relations are
<u>given</u>", [59] and on the other hand, <u>logical</u>, in which

"concepts, whencesoev   ,iven, are only <u>subordinated</u> to one anoth r, the lower to the hi h r (the common marks), and compared with one  noth r accordin  to the princi le of contradiction".[60]  In  oth works, then, the  rinci le of contradiction is held to be char cteristic of one use of the intellect, and in each c se, this is its  urely lo ical use.  But the relation of the  rinci le of contradiction to <u>time</u> is significantly different in each case.

In the <u>Inau ural Dissert tion</u> time is held to be intimately associated with the oper tions of the intellect in the use of the  rinci le of contradiction.

> Further, though time does not indeed prescribe laws to reason, it yet establishes the chief conditions by the help of which the mind can order its notions accordin  to the laws of reason.  Thus I cannot decide wheth r a thin  is impossible, except by predicatin  A and not-A of the same subject <u>at the  ame time</u>.   61

That Kant meant what he sai  can be seen from his repetition of the same point in the very place where he is at  ains to ex ose the errors due to the contamination of intellectual kno ledge by the sensitive in the metaphysical fallacy of subreption.  H re sensitive or phenomenal characteristics are attached to  urely intellectual conce ts in such a manner that  henomena are intellectualized, that is, as Kant w s later accusto-

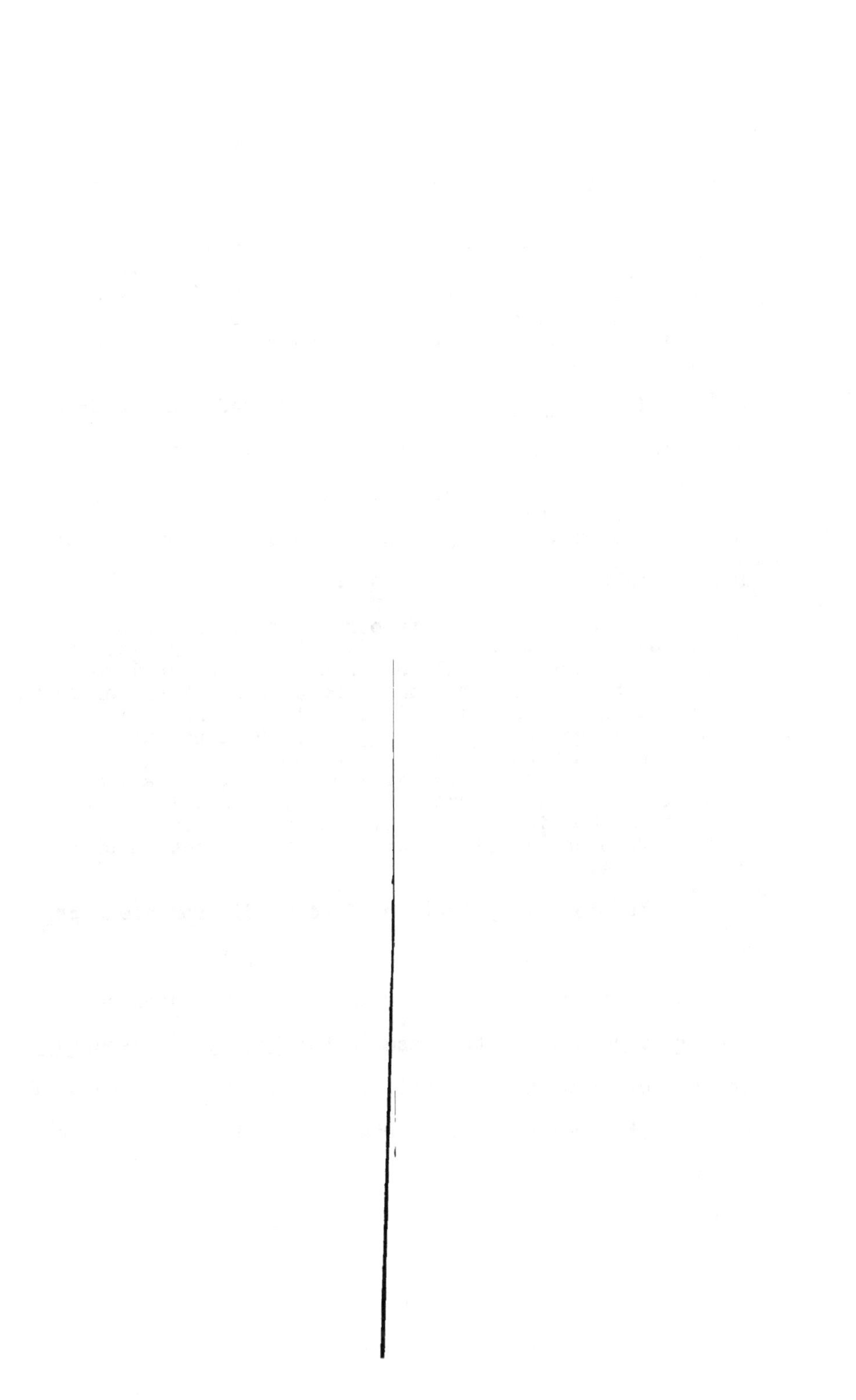

med to us it, or seen as things in themselves.

That is to say, our intellect recognises impossibility only where it can veri rly the simultaneous enunciation of two opposites about the same object, i.e. only where a contradiction occurs. The human intellect, therefore, can make no judgment of impossibility in cases in which this contradiction is not is not found. 62

In the _writing_, on the other hand, the doctrine that time "establishes one chief conditions by the help of which the mind can order its notions according to the laws of rea on", 63 is expressly repudiated. Thus of the law of contradiction Kant says that.

Although this famous principle is thus without content and merely form 1, it has sometimes been carelessly formulated in a manner which involves the quite unnecessary admixture of a synthetic element. The formula runs: It is impossible that somethin should at on_ and th _a_e time both be and not be... -the pro osition is modified by the condition of time... The principle of contradiction, however, as a merely lo ical principle, must not in any way limit its assertions to time-relations. The above formula is therefore completely contrary to the invention of the principle. 64

The logical principle of contr diction needs no help from time, and this being the case, it is apparent that time bears a different relation to the intellect in the _Critique_ than is the case in the _Inau ural Dissertation_. In the former work the intellectual functions of the self or subject, from which the principles which bring about the unity of nature must ultimately derive, are freed from any confusion with either of the two extensive continua

expresses this in the Inaugural Dissertation by saying
that "time approaches more nearly (than space) to a
universal, rational concept, in that it embraces absolutely everything within its survey".[5]   And in the
Critique Kant explains why the categories may be schematised by means of time-determinations, as follows:

> Now a transcendental determination of time
> is so far homogeneous with the category, which con-
> stitutes its unity, in that it is universal and
> rests upon an a priori rule. But, on the other hand,
> it is so far homogeneous with appearance, in that time
> is contained in every empirical representation of the
> manifold. 66

Both in the Inaugural Dissertation and the
Critique of Pure Reason Kant distinguishes between space
and time as forms of sensibility, and as pure intuitions.
The distinction between them, then, is a distinction between two different a priori formal conditions of sen-

It is neither substance nor accident nor relation,
but is a subjective condition, necessary owing to
the nature of the human mind, of the co-ordination
of all sensibles according to a fixed law; and it
is a pure intuition.        67

Kant describes space in almost identical language
after stating that "the concept of space is this pure
intuition", 68 and also "the fundamental form of all other
sensations", 69 Kant goes on to repeat what he has said
about time in almost identical terms.

> Space is not something objective and real,
> neither substance, nor accident, nor relation, but
> subjective and ideal; and, as it were, a schema,
> issuing by a constant law from the nature of the
> mind, for the connecting of all outer sensa what-
> soever.  70

Although there is a certain change in the distinction between space and time in the Critique of Pure
Reason, from that of the Inaugural Dissertation, they are
still distinguished in the same manner, namely, as forms
of sensibility. The change is due to Kant's sharper
realization of the difference between intuition and
thought. Hence in the Dissertation Kant could say that;

> So far is it from being possible that anyone
> should ever deduce and explain the concept of time by
> the help of reason, that the very principle of contra-
> diction presupposes it, involving it as a condition.
> For A and not-A are not incompatible unless they are
> judged of the same thing together (i.e., in the same
> time)...........  71

On the other hand, in the Critique Kant has completely

sever d any nece s ry  n inti  e c n ction  tw en the
peculiar function. of conce tu l t'inki   'n  intuition;
althou h, o. cour ,   stre ses their  io1 in . irical kno led c.  In eed, it is only bec'u-e  nt ^ s ' en
at  re^t ai  to isolate and examin the  eculi r nature
of each, and r ake cl 'r wh^t the function- o' ^ac' consist
in, th t he can  rc ent a clc-r acco nt o° th t unior.
T us, in t'e introductory rem rks to t'e Tr nscendental
Aesthetic, ' ^nt announces that "In t'e course of this
investi tion it will ' ^ foun  t at th  e are two  ure
forms o. sen j'l  intuition, servin  as  rinci les of
a priori kno' led e, namely, sp ce an  ti e", [72] and continue
on to present his ar umonts for this con ention, without
mentionin  any necessary rel tion o' on  o  th se  ure
intuitions, namely, time, to the o rations of the intellect.   e e phasize this point because we wish to
stress th t t'e sin ular role of time in the philoso hy
of Kant does not consi t in time enterin  into the
operations of the intellect as a condition o° them. The
princi le of individuation, an  its rel ted  rinciples,
must in the nature o. thin s b  consid rea  s distinct
from the medium to which it a plies.

The diff rences between space an  ti e in K nt's
philosophy, howev r, are not limited to their bein  dif-

...ent forms of sensibility. The similarities a differences for want correspond, in , o t o ch e
point o o .... o ction it ri o C. .
ro .

Space and ti e are both continua, or in Kant's
words, "space an' i e are quanta continua"[73], and therefore extensive. Space and ti are the two original
quanta of all our intuition"[74], but there is an intrinsic
difference between the in their extensiveness. "Time
is in itself a series, and indeed the formal condition
of all series'[75], but space, on the other hand, "is an
aggregate, not a series"[76]. By this Kant seems to mean
that space or spatial series has no intrinsic direction, for he say that"....in space, taken in now by
itself, there is no distinction between progress a regress"[77]. There is, however, a progress in the time-series
from past to present.

> The present moment can be regarded only as
> conditioned by past time, never as conditioning it,
> because this moment comes into existence only through
> past time, or rather through the passing of the re-
> ceding time. [78]

Kant clearly regards time as a series which has an
intrinsic sense of direction from past to future. Furthermore, he regards this series as deriving its intrinsic
direction from the fact that it has one end open to which

n w events are consequently initiated. 1 o  he uts
t is point in  a  of conditional     .  ti  ,
his  a   1  cl  .

> Time ve necessarily th in.            v n
> com let ly elapsed u  to the  iv n  o  t, an.  s boin
> it elf  iv n in t is co  l ted form.  This 'olds
> true,  v n thou h such co  l tely clapsed tim. is not
> determina le   us.  Bu since t     e i  ot the
> condition of our attainin  to the  re ent, it is a
> matt  o   ntire indi 'f  nce, in o   co   ehension
> of the latter, how we may think of future time, whether
> as comin  to    .  or  s  lovin  on to infinity.  e
> have, as it were, th  series $m$, $n$, $o$, in which $n$
> is  iven a  conditioned b, $m$,  n   t  the sam ti e
> as bein  the condition of $o$.  The series ascends from
> the  ro   the conditioned $n$  o $u$ ($l$, $k$, $i$, etc.),
> and also descends from the condition $n$ to the con-
> ditioned $o$ ($r$, _, $i$, _c.).   79

Time, for make, flow,  to  e e, "down ill",
from the past to the  re ent;  , , /  u  o n w events,
on into the future.

Space and time, however,    a     selves  re
not conce  u.  kand is e  ha tic on  u   oi  .  They  u t
therefore  e unique, havin  nothin  in co  on  ith  ch
other or  ith anyt in  else.  For i  th    anythin  in
common  ith anythin  else,   co  on elements would
provide a  asis for a discursive conce t.   ut it is
extremely di ficult to try to reconcile  ant's doctrine
that s ace an  tim   e i tuitions and hence sin ul r,
with his num rous state e tcs  so   their analo ous
properties.  To   cert in exte t t  i ficulty can  e

re ol ed.  or    l , h  u  re    o o eneous

anifold in    s ce or ti e i   e esul of

synthe is,  t, as  ton oints o t,    ex l n tion

of thi  c n   be  iven in the Transce  e al  esthetic,

where k nt   rim ily concerned with sensibility in

isol tion.

> urth m.o e,  ntil I a    ex lained his
> doc rine of synthesis, he  as to s eak as if t e
> unity o s ce   d tine were <u>iven</u> in i uition.
> It can, ho ev r,  . iven only because of a synthesis
> which o   not lo  to  n e. The necess ry
> synthetic unity of s ce (and o time) depends u on,
> and rre  o  , t  u e c e ories o  the un-
> derstandin .  ll this is omi t d from the  esthetic,
> but i s    to    u'   uch n omission is  fensible.
>  an ca no  ex lain his whole  hiloso hy t once.  80

Inso  r   the nalo i  te   rom thi  nity,

there is no neces ry inconsi tency  t  kan t  vie that

space and tine a e ure intuitions.   ut i ofa  as  ce

and ti c e of such a nature t    n an lo ous unity,

and co on conc ts, must be form d of th , they cannot

be consi ered uni ue.  s intuitions they would hen **have**

marked simil rities.  It is clear th t if th c te ories

of quantit are a lic ble to oth space and time, they

<u>i so facto</u> have that much in common.  nd it is abun-

dantly clear th  k nt did thin t  p c nd time

were capable of bein re resented in t  ame terms.

Besides those definite st ements to which we ave already

... ... ... ... " conc ... ... c ... n time,
as quanta, ... ... i ... _a priori_ in intuition, that is,
constructed, ... in respect of ... quality (... ure)
of the given, ... through number in their quantity only
(the ... synthesis of the homogeneous manifold)".[81]

Now it is ... that ... ... that there might be
two pure intuitions, which ... unique in themselves, yet have
something in common. This is apparently ... view.
Nevertheless, such a doctrine, if it is to avoid the contradiction ... ... of eclecticism which ... mentioned
above in ... ..., ... maintain that the essential of
either space or ... is omitted when they are represented
in similar concepts. Otherwise the essential o both
space and time will ... adequately ... re ented in the same
concepts and ... distinction ... een ... intuitions
will be unnecessary. One intuition, ... o t, would be
enough, for they would represent a common type of intuition even if there were a plurality o ther which dif-
fered in unessential ways. There would be no ... point
in distinguishing them than there would be in distinguishing
a multiplicity of separate intuitions of space, an' supposing them to be different kinds of intuition.

Nevertheless, Kant does distinguish between space
and time, not only in that time is all-pervasive in the

a here of sense, e a seen, a also in u t every-
thin t u is in ce is also in m , wi l states
or u l e i i lo . on ll ou lo e ne
in lic ion o t i latter point in subsequent sections.
I an hile it can c noted that these two points involve
one another. For if of lo is all-pervasive, in con-
ur distinction to space, it follows that something must
be in ti e alone. en it i eld, as Kant does, that
states peculiar to c eli such as t ou hts an feelings
are in ti e alone, this is a clear indication that Kant
has rejected the theory which we l elied above as
ossibility . i is theory is committed to attributing a
materialistic psychology, while Kant, as we shall see,
reject the possibility of any sort of science of
psychology entirely.

Kant's position is not, in itself, radically
different from that of Broad, for both of them, while
conscious of the fundamental distinction between space
and time, attempt to express this distinction by means
of spatial analogies. Time is distinguished from space
conceptually in that time is a series, which has an intrinsic direction. We have already expressed doubts as
to whether the difference between space and time is adequately expressed in these terms. Kant's denial that

[illegible] of criticism [illegible] particular[illegible] [illegible] that [illegible] distinction still involve[illegible] cit [illegible] [illegible] I [illegible] not have [illegible] [illegible] of [illegible] [illegible] [illegible] [illegible] [illegible], [illegible], [illegible] impossible to [illegible] [illegible] difference [illegible] [illegible] temporal series and [illegible] spatial series. [illegible] points [illegible] have already mentioned concern [illegible] [illegible] distinction between space and [illegible] [illegible] consequence of any such view as the one we have designated as [illegible]ility. [illegible] [illegible] recognition of non-spatial [illegible] [illegible] [illegible] enough to ensure this. But further consider[illegible] associated with his Copernican revolution led Kant to adopt the theo[illegible] we have called [illegible]ility B. Before discus[illegible] in this, however, it is necessary to accept a clarification of what Kant meant by inner and outer sense.

CHAPTER

ANTHROPOLOGY OF      C

## 2. Inner and Outer Sense

Kant's doctrine of inner and outer sense is difficult, and while we shall present what we hope is a
consistent and intelligible interpretation thereof, it
cannot be romantically asserted that this presentation
is what Kant had in mind.  It is to be feared that
Kant's terminology in regard to this doctrine is not
entirely consistent, and although this does not entitle
us to conclude _ipso facto_ that the doctrine is thus necessarily inconsistent with itself, it does make it hard
to know whether one is understanding Kant rightly.
Nevertheless, the interpretation to be here expounded is
based on documentary evidence, and makes it possible to
view in a new light some puzzling features of the
critical philosophy which seem inexplicable according
to alternative treatments, for example, the account of
the schematism of the categories.

Kant's distinction between inner and outer sense
is based, at bottom, on his belief that not all the matter
of experience is given in spatial relations, and this
insight he expressed as early as the _Inaugural Dissertation,_

sayin  of time, th t it "embraces  osoluely ev rythin

within  ts survey, namely, sp ce itself,  n  in addition

the acci  nts which are not comprehended in   ce-
relations, such as the thor hts of the soul'.   This in-

trouuces anoth r aspect of the distinction which Kant

also anticipates in th  Inau ural 'i sert ion, name-

ly, that inn r sen e is bound u  wit  the st  es or re-

presentations of the soul, and th t outer sense i  as-

sociated with spatially extended objects.

> Of these concepts, the one (i.e. space)
> pro erly concerns the intuition of an object,
> the other (i.e. time) a state, namely, th t of re-
> presentation.  83

Kant is not very explicit concemin  what the

term "sta e" com rises in thi  cont xt.  In one  l ce,

however, he seems to indicate that he  oes not mean

what would now be t rmed a fective states, i.e. feelin s.

> . . . it is es ecially  elev nt to observe
> that everything in our knowled e which belon s to
> intuition -- feelin  of  leasure and  ain, and the
> will, not being knowled e, are excluded -- contains
> nothin  out  ere rel tions.  84

Kant is here referrin  to  no le  e, ho ev r,

anc, as we shall see, the a pearances of  he inner states

of the soul are not objects of knowled e.  In other

places Kant definit ly includes thou hts an   eelin s

as inn r states.   But the catalo uin  of all th  inner

sense comprises may not be necessary as long as the
basis for the distinction between inner and outer sense
can be made clear. Unfortunately, Kant presents the
distinction in a very brief form. Inner and outer sense
are described as means whereby we become conscious of
inner states and outer objects, but Kant does not el-
aborate on the nature of these means.

> By means of outer sense, a property of our
> mind, we represent to ourselves objects as outside
> us, and all without exception in space. In space
> their shape, magnitude, and relation to one another
> are determined or determinable. Inner sense, by
> means of which the mind intuits itself or its inner
> state, yields indeed no intuition of the soul itself
> as an object; but there is nevertheless a determinate
> form (namely, time) in which alone the intuition of
> inner states is possible, and everything which belongs
> to inner determinations is therefore represented in
> relations of time. 86

This passage, however, yields us one point of
importance to which we can hold fast, namely, that whatever else Kant may mean by inner and outer sense, the
former contains time-relations and the latter space-
relations. But it should be added that Kant makes no
mention of a mutual exclusion of the two. Although this
would seem to be a natural inference, it may be, as with
many of Kant's terms, dangerous to jump to conclusions.
As it turns out, there is actual evidence that they are not
mutually exclusive. To be more explicit, it is not the
case that what is intuited in inner sense in time-

ut since all representations, whether they
have for their objects outer things or not, belong in
themselves, as determinations of the mind, to our
inner state; and since this inner state stands under
the formal condition of inner intuition, and so be-
longs to time, time is an a priori condition of all
appearance whatsoever.        87

Kant makes the same point in terms of empirical

knowledge:

        All increase in empirical knowledge, and every
advance of perception, no matter what the objects
may be whether appearances or pure intuitions, is
nothing but an extension of the determination of
inner sense, that is, an advance in time.  This advance in time determines everything and is not itself determined through anything further.    88

Thus, as Kant puts it, "There is only one

whole in which all our representations are contained,
                                              89
namely, inner sense and its a priori form, time".  Inner

sense with its form, time, seems, as did time in the

Inaugural Dissertation, to be "absolutely primary in the

domain of sense".

There is, then, some reason to believe that what

Kant means by inner sense is consciousness, in general,

of anything that may be an object for us.  This empirical

consciousness, of course, must be distinguished from the

transcendental unity of apperception, through which alone

A perception and its synthetic unity is,
indeed, very far from being identical with inner sense

Inner sense, in this meaning of the panorama of
changing conscious states, may be entitled, says Kant,
empirical apperception.

Consciousness of self according to the determinations of our state in inner perception is
merely empirical, and always changing. No fixed and
abiding self can present itself in this flux of
inner appearances. Such consciousness is usually
named inner sense, or empirical apperception. 91

It is to be noted that Kant says it is no fixed
and abiding self that can present itself, but not necessarily no fixed and abiding appearance. This interpretation of inner sense requires, however, that representations of outer sense be included within inner
sense, and this seems to be flatly contradicted by some
of Kant's statements, for example, "Time cannot be outwardly intuited, any more than space can be intuited as
something in us", 92 and:

Time is nothing but the form of inner sense,
that is, of the intuition of ourselves and our inner
state. It cannot be a determination of outer appearances; it has to do neither with shape nor position, but with the relation of representations in
our inner state. 93

It should be noted, however, that Kant does not
here specifically say that outer sense cannot be in-

cluded within _inner sense_, but only t'  u _time_ c nnot  be
outwardly intui_d, an  c nnot be     t rmin _ion of outer
a pea' nces. In  'ort, e _  ot   'i  of out r and
inner sense a_ all _er se_, but o_ t'e  _nner in whic  we
can intuit ti e.  It  s only y ne ns o_ n inf_ nce
th t wo c n con tru  th se st _ _ nt  to  n t' t outer
sense, wit'h it_  atial r L tions, cannot be  included in inn  r sen_  with its tem oral relations.  It is,
of course, perf ctly obviou  that K nt n ed  ter or l relations to obt in in the s here of        ll e t ended
objects.  C h  wi e, he coul  not  os ibly answer the
que tion "How i3 pure science of nature possible?", [94]
which is one of 'his avo ed purposes.

 I  we constru  inner sense to mean empirical
a perception, we may still maintain that time cannot be
outwa dly intuited, in the sense that time c nnot be intuited in that which is purely spatial.  Likewise, time
would not then be a determination of outer a pear nces.
Outer sense, by this token, would be a t rm standing
for our bil ty to a prehend obj cts in spatial relations, and only in spatial rel tions.  hat is apprehended in out r sense would be an abstraction from
inner sense.  This is, p rhaps, only a lo ic 1 result of
distinguishin  between space and time as two different

ure intuitions. If space certain is here wide and
distinct way of intuition, it follows th  determinations
peculiar to the one will not be peculiar to the other.

K nt's distinction between inner and outer sense
thus seems to amount to this. When we are perceiving
anything, we are also empirically conscious th t _we_
are perceiving it. Whatever is given i always given
to us with our peculiar mode of sensibility. In the
totality of all th t  experience, however, some things
are given, which, considered in  ntur ction by themselves, are purely in spatial relations; other things
are given which are purely in temporal relations, namely,
certain mental st tes, states which we clearly and
intuitively recognize as non-spatial.  ut nothing is given
to us which is neither in space or ti e.  Nor is anything ever given which is not in time, but only in space.

Hence "inner sense" inclu es two meanings, or
to put it otherwise, covers two ar s of representations,
which are not necessarily mutually exclusive.  On the
one hand, inner sense may mean whatever pertains to my
non-spatial mental states.  This is a narrow meaning of
inner sense.  On the other hand, inner sense may mean all
my experience of whatever kind.  This is  ide meaning.
It is not certain that Kant does not alt rnate these
meanings.  It is fairly certain that he uses "inner sense"

in the wide meaning often enough to make the meaning

of it clear, as can be seen from the fore oin quotations,

as well as the following:

> Whatever the origin of our representations,
> whether they are due to the influence of outer things,
> or are produced through inner causes, whether they
> arise _a priori_ or being appearances have an empirical
> origin, they must all as modifications of the mind,
> belong to inner sense.  All our knowledge is thus
> finally subject to time, the formal condition of
> inner sense.   95

> . . . appearances are not things in them-
> selves, but are the mere play of our representations,
> and in the end reduce to determinations of inner sense. 96

Yet Kant also often uses the term 'inner sense"

to mean whatever pertains to non-spatial "states", and

distinguishes these from the contents of outer sense:

> In outer sense we find no other outer effects
> save changes of place, and no forces except mere ten-
> dencies which issue in spatial relations as their
> effects. Within us, on the other hand, the effects
> are thoughts, among which is not to be found any re-
> lation of place, motion, shape, or other spatial de-
> termination . . .  97

The distinction between inner sense is what has

been here called the narrow meaning, and outer sense,

thus seems to rest solely on the distinction between

space and time themselves.  Inner sense contains that

which is only in time-relations, and outer sense that

which which as well as being in time is also in space.

           ᴜ  ᴄ nsc n ᴄnᴜᴧl o  ᴄᵗ  ᴜ  ually un-
known in reᵴ ᴄt to inn r  ᴜ  to out ᴧ intuition.
 ᴜt it ıs not o ᴛhı tᵗ t    ᵌ h ᴜ  ᴏᴄᴋınᴜ,
but of the ᴜ ırıᴄ l object, which ıᴊ ᴄ lled an
extᴜrnᴄl objᴜᴄt ᵌ it ıᴜ re re ented in ᴄᴘ ᴄe,
and ᴜn innᴱr ooj ᴄt il it iᴊ re resenᴛed only in
its tı ᴜ-ᴧ l tio s. ᴊ ᴜlthᴼᴜ ᴜ ᴄ ᴜ ᵗti ᴇ,
hoᴠevᴜr, ıᴊ to ᴜ iouᴜn ᴄave in us.  98

In trᴠin  to ex lain more fully th ᵌiᴜfᴜᴱnc

ᴜetween reᵢresent tions ᴧhich ᴬre in inn r sunᵗe ᴄnd

those which are in outer sense, a distinction ᴠhich seems

to rᴜquirᴜ ᴜn intuitive ᴜrasᴊ of the diᴄfernᴄnce betᴠeen

space and timo thᴜ ᴜselves, Kᴄnt alloᴡs himself sorᴜe rather

picturesque lᴜnᵢua e:

           ᴜattᴜr, th refoᴄᴇ, doᴇᴄ ᴜot ᴜᴜᴜn a kind of
suᴊsᴛᴜnce quiᴜᴜ distiᴄct ᴜd hetᴇro ᴊneouᴊ from
the oᴜject of innᴄᴠ sense (the soul), ᴜut only the
distinctive nᴄture of those aᴜᴘeᴜrances of ooᴊ ᴜcts--
in themselves unknown to us--the represcntationᴊ
oᴜ ᴧhich ᴠᴊ call outᴜr aᴜ comᴘᴄred with those we
count as belonᴜin  to innᴜᴼ sᴜnse, althouᴜh, like
ᴜll other tho ᴜhts these outᴜr re resentations ᵌ
belonᴜ only to the thinkinᴜ subject.  ᴛheᴜ have,
indeed, ᴛhis dece tive ᴘroᴘerty that, representinᴜ
objects in space, they detach themselves aᴊ it were
from the soul, ᴼnᵌ appear to ᴛoᴠ ᴼ outᴄiᴜe it.  99

If we beᴜin ᴠith ᴠhat ᴜiᴛht bᴜ ᴄ lled "total ex-

porience", innᴜᴧ sense in the narrow me ning of non-

spatial thouᴜhts flittiᴜ throuᴛh tᴜe soul, is an ab-

straction from total experience.  Siᴧilarly, outer

sense, concᴜived as aᴘᴘᴱarances wᴜich ᴜᴇ only sᵢatially

extᴜnded iᴊ ᴄlso ᴜn abstraction from totᴜl ᴄxᴘerience.

In this mᴜanin  oᴄ "innᴱr" and "outer" it woulᴜ be quite

## 109

100

... ..., t i n ot b ou l intui e any
th n c c n i ai d s o c i in us",
out h e abstruction ill av r lev ce only for the
ure intui io c d , , hey will oe
useful in ex l ain t tuo b i of sensibility.
They vill o ful in x lain u iv rsal
sensi l ch r c istic o ll ex ri nce atsoever,
of _possible_ ex rience. or that, a i e n aning of
"inn r" and "out r" sense will uired. In th
context, inn r en will turn out to b coextensive
with all rience whatsoev r; and ou r sense vill en-
compass re r nt ions hich, a rt of i er sense,
are _i o cto_ in time-r lations, na distinctively
characterized by the f ct hat t ey e lso in s ce.

I is a ja ent that k nt s thi kin in his doctrine of inn r sense, o the paramount i o ance of the
train of non-s atial re resent tions in our a rehension
of time, a ac which has oeen reco nized by some riters
on psycholo y. For exa ple, in Stout's _Manual of
Psychology_, written, as the author points out, from the
" enetic point of view", we find the following statement:

The a prehension o c or l l tions, as
they exist for human consciousness, is an extremely

co l   c  c o   nt l  ev lo  nt.   l  rt
layed in   ty cr rs of fr e i     o  e-
o in nt i  o   ce.   101

Si ilaily,    t  c  to       i  attention to
tr ins o ide s            t  v rything th t is in
inn r ense, is in co    nt flux".   I nt hol  these
ch n es in in    es to    o co innous th t "Io
fixed an  b in      c  r ent itn lf in this flux
of inn r a earenc s'.    Put the train of ideas throu h
which wo   c consci s c  ot  our  hnno enal selves and
of ten or l series c niot   o separ tod e ce t abstr ctly, fro  tho e a e   nc s which we  ntitle outer,
a point whic  I nt im  lf  ahns in  yin  th t "the
represent ions o  the ou    senses constitute the
proper mat rial  ith which  e occu y our ind".   104
Accordin  to otout, t    n ins of ide s, the  ort of
thin  which l nt  ou l  ay co  ris s in r s nse in the
narrow me nin  of th  t n , is absolutely indis ensable
to the ap rehension of time.

Without  uch tr ins there coul  be no such
thing as the definite apprehension of  tine-series,
having a distin uishable beginnin  and end, connected
by a train of int rmediate events, e ch h vin  its
own  osition det m ined by its rel tion to other
events which h ve come before and  ft r it.  105

Perhaps the di ficulty we h ve in unde standing
Kant's theory of inn r s ns  is due to our not taking

...iously ... it ... whole intellect,
which ... co ... upon. It ... indeed a
f ct ... ithou ... r in f ... ir ... constant flux
of inn ... (in ... ro ... nin ), ... co l ... io
a ... nsion ... t , ... ou ... in t' t h nt
shoul have ...tended ... i ... o ... ure to include all tu - l ioi ... ov r. If, is Stout points
out, without trains of ideas, ... ou ... no apprehension of in -s ies t e ... utev ... i e-s i ... e do
in ct appre end, o ... xa le, a ti e-s ries in spatially
ex ended objects, oul i o cto in some ay involve
inner sen... Thus, it voul ... only ec u e did not
ake ai psycholo ic l ct seriously enou , did not,
that is, ...e the generality of it, ... ... ve woul ... u ose
t at time-series of outer a e ances did ot involve
inner sense, and dra t c inco ect conclusion ... a
theory of tine ased on inn. sense coul. k. 10 ccount
of such outer time-series. het'r or not Stout's
contention is the whole truth about our a rehension
of time is not to the resent pur ose to discuss.
Nevertheless, sequential ex e ience whether of i eas or
of other psycholo ical states see s to ... sine ua
non of any theory of the a rehension of time. rtlett,
who su ests that "Very likely it is true that the akin

o^ ti - i.ti ctio s is, p^yc'olo ic'lly, ^un    ent lly
soci lly 'et rmin      onse",      ^lso ^ y  .h t one of
the  ^s nti^ls of ^  ^yc'olo ic l  .neory o. t.e ar-
 ^ehension o  t.    ^ 'the form tio  ^' o^ n'zed c'ains
o^ s^^c_ siv  acti itie  t] ou h the o  r tion o^ some
 ^iolo ic^l o^  ^ycholo ic l int^_e^t".      ^uccessiveness
of p^ych^olo ic l st. es, t]hen, i^ intimately associated
with the ^nprehen^ion of ti^e, ^nd this is, ^ bottom,
t.e  ^oi^t to ^' 1ch ' nt 'as dr^wn at^ention.  It is here
th t K.nt ^n^ the  sycholo i^t ^art ^ays.  ^or K nt the
^act of t'^ succe^sion o^ ^sycholo ic^l st   es ^s only
ex^lic ^le in t^rms of ^ transcendent l an lysis of 'uman
kno^l^d e,  ^rt of which n^ce sarily de ls ^ith ^ensi-
bility.  ^o  th^ ^sycholo ist int^ est t^^minates in
the det r^in^tion of the f ct and its pl^ce in t.e theory
of e. iric l psycholo y.

Kant' ^ ^rticular int_re^t in ^rawin  a dis-
tinctio^ bet^_en inn ^ ^n  o t.r s_n e necessit^tes a
third . e ^in , not inco ^ati'le ^ith, .^t differ nt from
the others, ^hic^ h^ ives to ^hese ^ rms.  This third
meanin  i  a pa_ently o.t^i^ed by abstr_ctin   ure re-
l^tio^s fro.n inn^. an  out _ sense in the ^ider me nin^.
H_^e  e is not  _ ^in  o^ in ^r an^ ov^t^r ^nse as the
whole of a ^e^rances  n^ the spatial a^pear^nces within

t    ol ,                              li  i    h
m    r (o    ... ... ;  i    ... o i.. r
a.. o          l          l i... .

1                       ... l .  '
o .. l  ...  ...    (.) ...-3   l  ..e-
s... io i.. j-  i ,    (_) ...rl ... nt ions
also in ti ...  ...   ,      ... i l   t
ar   o i l    or   c   i..n (_).  ut in t'is
conc.. t  ...  i.. i  ...       n ol
the  t o  ...  ...  ll   ...  . I' b-
stre ction .  ...  ...  tt , o   , i..   e
will be the net-ork of ti e-rel.. ions t'rou..out ossible s. ... ce,  .. our ... ... ll .. ... net-ork
of s.atial rel.. ion t..o..o t o ..iol ... ience.
because i..  ... ... h.. o  conc.. ... .. in o  the
"sum of all re.. ... ions" cc.. i.. n ..ed o  re.re-
sent.. ion.  ich  ... both in ...  ... l ..d to o..l relations, .. ... ... token, inn  ense in ..i o..e
abstr ct  ..nin, ill cont.. in ... o..l rel..io.. t ich
relate re.. ... e.. ion.. which ... lo in   ti l  .l.tions.
Thus, .. termin.. ion o  ...  ..ro.. ..  ... r.s, n ..tal
unity o a. erception ..ill   fect ov..   .ea  nce..

    Kant speaks o.. the i e..lit, o..  ..' out   ..
109
inner sense",    just as he asserts the e..irical reality

o  .e  i  .  ..  .  .  .sc  .  l  . li./.  In
co..i. ti.  .  .  .  . rtion, .  .c. o. .ne
1 .t , . .  .. . o  1  .  .. outer
sen.e  i  .1 .io..

> relations. . . .This also holds true of inner sense
> . . . .c u.e ..  .. .. .  .el  . .ot . .. . re-
> present.tions . . . itself contains only relations
> . . . 111

'1 .c, .in 11. ,  ..  .  .  .  .c .c loc-
.l. of i.. .  . .  .  .  .  .'. .n. ne' to .c-
co. lish .h. .ur.o. . o .h. _Cri.i.. o. ..e ___on_.
Inn.. sense  s .r.nscen .n..lly i .1  .  .. . .. .e
n.tvo.. o ..i.-..l.ions t.ro..out .o.i.l. e...i.nce.
Oulcr .u. .  . no. or' of s.tinl .l..ions .hroug.-
out .o .i l. e..cri.nce, ... .he o'j.c.s .h.. l .ed in
s. c. .  1 o  1 .ed in .l.c in inn. en.e, (as tr.n-
scendentally id..l), .bec.use,  Ju.t as I . . .ay a priori
that all ou. . . . .e ..nces ... in ..ce . . . I c.n lso
say, .ron. .he .rinci.l. of in..r .en.c, .. . .11
a.pe. .nc. . ...soev.. , t.. t . , .ll ol.j.c. .. .he
senses, .e in .i..c, ... .ce .il. . .. i. t.. e-re-
lations".  112  Inn.r .nd out.r .en.e, .h.n, lik. ti.e and
space, a.e e..iric lly r. .1, .ut tr.nscen..ent lly ideal,
or .s K nt ut. it, t.ey .e nothin. in t e..elves.  '.he
distinction botw.en inn . and outer sense re..ts o. the

f[illegible] [illegible] [illegible] e [illegible] [illegible] e-
iric l [illegible] [illegible] [illegible] ns
of di[illegible] [illegible] 1, [illegible] ded
o'ject , [illegible], 1[illegible] 1 [illegible].

[illegible] 1 [illegible]. [illegible] 1 [illegible] I
myself, and both, indeed, upon the imm[illegible]e witness
o[illegible] y [illegible]f-co[illegible]c[illegible] n [illegible]. [illegible] on[illegible] [illegible]c[illegible] is
that the re[illegible]resent tion of myself, as the thin[illegible]in[illegible]
s[illegible]j[illegible]ct, [illegible]o to [illegible] [illegible]n [illegible]o[illegible], [illegible]l [illegible] represent tions which mark extended [illegible]ein[illegible]s belon[illegible] <u>also</u>
to out [illegible] s[illegible] se. 113

[illegible] th[illegible] [illegible]uo[illegible] [illegible]io[illegible] [illegible]i[illegible]c [illegible], [illegible] e [illegible],
on the e[illegible] ic l l[illegible] 1, 'o[illegible] o [illegible]h[illegible] o[illegible] s [illegible] nd
[illegible] [illegible] par[illegible]nce[illegible], [illegible] [illegible] [illegible]c[illegible][illegible]l[illegible] i[illegible]clu[illegible] t[illegible]ose
"u on [illegible] [illegible] [illegible] of [illegible] [illegible]lf-conscio[illegible]n[illegible][illegible]".
In [illegible] [illegible] [illegible]o c[illegible] [illegible] id in[illegible] [illegible] [illegible], [illegible]en, the [illegible]ph[illegible]sis
shoul[illegible] [illegible] on <u>[illegible]</u>, [illegible] for [illegible] t, [illegible]h[illegible] [illegible] [illegible]r s ste[illegible] to be
n [illegible] [illegible]or t[illegible] c[illegible] cit[illegible] to [illegible][illegible]se [illegible]ti[illegible]l rel[illegible]tions and
the ca[illegible]cit[illegible] to [illegible][illegible]se te[illegible]or[illegible]l [illegible]l ions, re[illegible]ectively.
[illegible]e must [illegible]i [illegible]ll our [illegible]rc[illegible]tion[illegible], [illegible][illegible]t [illegible] e c[illegible]ll [illegible]em
inn[illegible]r or out[illegible]r, [illegible] a con[illegible]cio[illegible]n[illegible][illegible] only o[illegible] [illegible][illegible] is
depende t on our [illegible]en[illegible]i[illegible]ility".   Outer o[illegible]ject[illegible] are re-
[illegible]r[illegible]se[illegible][illegible]io[illegible], "[illegible]hich [illegible][illegible] entitle[illegible] out[illegible] [illegible]c[illegible] [illegible] they
de[illegible]end on [illegible]h[illegible] c[illegible]ll 'outer sense', <u>ho[illegible]e intuition</u>
<u>i[illegible] [illegible] ce</u>"; [illegible] [illegible]epre[illegible]nt tion is an "<u>inn[illegible]r o[illegible]ject</u> i[illegible] it
is re[illegible]re[illegible]nte[illegible] only i[illegible] its tir[illegible][illegible]l tions".   T[illegible]us, in
the final [illegible]nalysis, inn[illegible]r and out[illegible] [illegible] n [illegible]u[illegible]t be

114

115

116

f[illegible] l [illegible]i[illegible]t[illegible]on [illegible] [illegible]e. [illegible]e-
iric[illegible]l [illegible]li[illegible] [illegible]. [illegible] [illegible]he [illegible]ns
of di[illegible] i[illegible] [illegible] [illegible]1, [illegible] ll [illegible] [illegible]ded
o'ject[illegible], [illegible] i[illegible] [illegible] [illegible], [illegible] 1[illegible], 1 [illegible].

[illegible] 1 [illegible]i[illegible] [illegible] 1[illegible] I
myself, [a]nd both, [i]ndeed, upon the immedi[at]e witness
o[f] [m]y [s]el[f]-con[s]ci[ous]n[es]s. [Th]e [p]oi[nt] [illegible] [illegible]c[illegible] is
that t[h]e re[p]resent[a]tion of myself, as the thinkin[g]
s[u]bj[e]c[t], [illegible]lo[n] to i[n] [illegible]n [illegible]o[illegible], [illegible]l[illegible] represent[a]tions which [m]ark extended bein[g]s belon[g] also
to ou[r] [illegible]s[e]se. 113

[illegible] th[illegible] [illegible]u[illegible]io[illegible]i[illegible]ic[illegible], [illegible] [illegible]e[illegible],
on the e[illegible]i[illegible]ic[illegible]l[illegible]l[illegible]l, o [illegible] o[illegible] [illegible][illegible] o[illegible] [illegible] [illegible]nd
[illegible] [illegible] [illegible]ar[illegible]nce[illegible], [illegible][illegible] [illegible] c[illegible]s[illegible]lly i[illegible]clu[illegible] t[h]ese
"u[illegible]o[illegible] [illegible][illegible]i[illegible] [illegible][illegible] [illegible] of [illegible] [illegible]l[illegible]-cons[illegible]io[illegible]n s[illegible]".
I[n] [illegible]ef[illegible][illegible] [illegible]o [illegible] [illegible] [illegible] inn[illegible] [illegible]e[illegible]e, [illegible]e[illegible], t[h]e e[illegible]ph[illegible]sis
shoul[illegible] [illegible] o[illegible] ___, [illegible]for [illegible][illegible]t, [illegible]h[illegible] [illegible] [illegible]r s[illegible]n[illegible] to be
n[illegible] o[illegible] [illegible]o[illegible] [illegible]'[illegible] c[illegible] cit[illegible] to s[illegible][illegible]e [illegible]ti[illegible]l rel[illegible]tions [illegible]nd
the c[illegible][illegible]cit[illegible] to s[illegible][illegible]se t[illegible][illegible]or[illegible]l [illegible][illegible]l[illegible]ions, re[illegible]pectively.
[illegible]e must [illegible]i[illegible] [illegible]ll o[illegible]r [illegible]rce[illegible]tion[illegible], "[illegible][illegible]t [illegible] [illegible] c[illegible]ll [illegible]em
inn[illegible]r or out[illegible]r, [illegible][illegible] a con[illegible]cio[illegible]n[illegible][illegible][illegible] onl[illegible] o[illegible] [illegible][illegible] i[illegible]
[illegible]epende[illegible]t on o[illegible]r [illegible]e[illegible]i[illegible]ilit[illegible]". 114 Out[illegible]r o[illegible]je[illegible][illegible] a[illegible]e re-
[illegible]r[illegible]se[illegible]t[illegible]io[illegible], "[illegible]ich [illegible] [illegible]ntitle[illegible] [illegible]u[illegible][illegible] [illegible][illegible]c[illegible][illegible][illegible] they
de[illegible]e[illegible]d on [illegible]h[illegible] [illegible] c[illegible]ll 'outer [illegible]ense', [illegible]h[illegible][illegible] intuition 115
i[illegible] [illegible][illegible]ce[illegible]"; [illegible] [illegible]epre[illegible][illegible]nt[illegible]tion i[illegible] an "inn[illegible]r o[illegible]ject i[illegible] it 116
is re[illegible]re[illegible]nte[illegible] onl[illegible] i[illegible] it[illegible] ti[illegible][illegible]-[illegible][illegible]l[illegible]tions". Th[illegible]s, in
the fin[illegible]l [illegible]nalysi[illegible], inn[illegible]r and o[illegible]t[illegible] [illegible][illegible]n[illegible] mu[illegible]t be

arded as aspects of possible experience, "the objective
n of experience in general, (which) contains all
thesis that is required for knowledge of objects". 117

One further point concerning inner sense remains
be dealt with.  As empirically real, inner sense refers
the network of time-relations throughout possible ex-
ience, but the inner sense to which Kant refers in
explanations of the conditions of the possibility of
s experience cannot be a network of relations, but
t be the pure intuition of time itself.

> Apperception and its synthetic unity is,
> indeed, very far from being identical with inner sense
> The former, as the source of all combination, applies
> to the manifold of intuitions in general, and in the
> guise of the categories, prior to all sensible in-
> tuition, to objects in general.  Inner sense, on the
> other hand, contains the mere form of intuition, but
> without combination of the manifold in it, and there-
> fore so far contains no determinate intuition, which
> is possible only through the consciousness of the
> determination of the manifold by the transcendental
> act of imagination. . .118

Just as the reproductive imagination presup-
119
as a productive imagination, a priori,  so our em-
ical inner sense presupposes a pure inner sense, which
tains a manifold, the content of the pure intuition of
e, capable of determination in accordance with the
egories.

> The understanding does not, therefore, find
> in inner sense such a combination of the manifold, but
> produces it, in that it affects that sense.   120

After unfolding so many different possible meanings of the distinction between inner and outer sense, it
may be advisable to sum them up.  Starting at the transcendental level and working down, inner sense may be
regarded as that which contains or comprises the pure
intuition of time; outer sense is that which constitutes
the pure intuition of space.  As such, inner and outer
sense are separable presuppositions of experience in
general.  But although they are both a priori presuppositions of experience in general, they are not related
to experience in the same way.  The form of inner sensibility, namely, time, is that in which all appearances
whatsoever are ordered; the form of outer sensibility is
that in which only those appearances called spatial are
ordered.  Inner sense relates to all experience; outer
sense to only a part of it.  And the recognition of the
difference between inner and outer sense, respectively,
depends on the intuitive grasp of time and space, themselves.

Considering the whole of possible experience,
the "one nature",  of which Kant never doubts the existence, inner sense must be regarded as identical with
the temporal aspect of the whole of it.  The advance of
perception is a revelation of what is in inner sense,

[illegible] [illegible] (_____ _ _ 11 _______ 10 )".[122] In
[illegible], [illegible] [illegible] [illegible] to e
the tot[a]l[ity] of [a]l[l] [intr]ic[a]lly [re]l[ated] [phenome]n[on]s, [w]hich
in t[he] [a]l[l] [illegible] [phe]n[omen]a[l] [illegible]",[123]
[a]n[d] [illegible] [the] [pr]e[sent] a[s] [ a ] [i]n[tuit]i[on], [ ] in [a]ll perce[p]tio[n] [a]n[d] [p]o[s]ition". In [th]i[s] [directi]on of inner
[sens]e, o[ ] [illegible] [in]t[uit]i[on] [illegible] [ ] t[ ] [o]f [i]ner
[sens]e, [w]o[rk] [illegible] [ ] [illegible] [a]o [ ] [fina]lly in [p]itin[g]
ours[el]v[es], [ ] [a]ll [as] [ th]s no[t]e of [i]ntuition in
[s]er[ia]s [ ] [ c ] [ ] [li]k[ew]ise [ ] [a]o ou[r] [fa]cilty of
c[oex]en[si]n [a]ll ou[t]er in[tu]itions'.[125] [Emp]irically ex-
[te]rn[al] [ob]j[ec]t [ ] [w]it[hi]n [ ] c[ ] [ ] [ fo u]n in
[sp]ace", [ ] [ ] [ ] i[s] [ ] o[ ] [ ] i[n]tuition [w]hich
[w]e c[a]ll ou[r] [ ]".[127] [Th]us, [f]or [u]s, in [ ] [sen]s[e in] its [s]ide,
concr[et]e r[ ] [ ] [s]o [t]i[ ] [ ] [ ] [o]f [p]heno[m]ena, [a]ll
o[f] which i[s] in [t]i[me], [an]d wit[h]in [t]i[t] [h]ole, ou[t]e[r] [s]ense
co[m]p[r]i[s]s [ ] [o]s[ ] [ ] [ou]r [s]ess [w]hich, [ ] [w]ell [ ] [u]i[n]g in
time, [ar]e 1[ ]o in [a] ce.

[A]s we h[ave] [a]lre[a]dy [n]o[te]d, [an] [abstra]ction is
[m]ade [fro]m [a]ll the [i]nt[uit]i[on] of [s]e[ns]ation, [inner] [and] ou[t]er
sense [w]ill co[m]p[r]i[se] [in]t[er] [o]r [suc]ce[ss]or [a]l [and] [spa]tial re-
l[a]tions, respectively, perv[a]din[g] [th]e [p]heno[m]enal [w]orld.

ll ,                                              r

,                                                          ur

in  il  , " 1 l            e

i n   cc      ,       ,

t    i  o  o      i  l i   i  .    128

In     i ,       i  ,      ,  con-

cious  ,       ,    c  c       1    i ed.

"All t     l   o in      ".  I       this    129

m  i      1          c ,-""  I

n o ject             ll i     l   form

of im       '.    o   ,            rrow    130

meanin i  "                        e

me     o  intrin ic ll        1         e

h   , t  l                    o lif-

n        i   r           c   un c  n  s,

i                      ions in    he-

nomenal o l  .   l                e i   nii com-

ris   ll       c , i       t  rro   ing

co  i           li  on   il o     , e  c ,

tc., o    l       ou             o ,

s ti l       u   i l              ng

o  , o   i   ts         tion t t

all  ie  ic i co  in  i     , (i      ide

meanin ),    u  inc  e in  r  e   in   n  o   ning,

[illegible] . . .

[illegible] 'I' [illegible]
sense in ti.., ..nd object. in ... c.. .. d ..e, are
.. ...i..lly ... ...ti... ... ..., ...ey ..e
not for t.. .. r...son thou.ht.s ..ein.. i.._erent
.. .. . 131

[illegible]posed ..o inner ..se in ... .. o.. ..ning
i.. o..... ... .. in ... ... r c. ... .., ou.. ..jects
..i..i.. ... ..t.l l....ns, _it ... ...ill..i..s_ only.
..s .ch, ...t..lly, ..me is ..ot .. c..t..n ..to t..n,
... ... ... ..o ..ut.o ..., is ... ...n ...er
..i.. ... ... ...io., ... it ... l..ion c.. r..
132
p.ese..t..i.. ... ... ..u..e. ... c..nt i..,
..e.., ...l.i... ... ... ...i.. ... ..ol..ly
..is..nc.. ..o... o... ..i...., ... ... ...2 o.. ..ce
..n.. the ____ o ...c, (ou... ... ... ...t..n ...
..n .o.. ., ...t co...c...l..), ... ...t..t ... .ocher.
I.... ... ..c.. ..nse in ... ... ...o.. ...: ...th
..s..ct.ol ..o.. co..o..e ex...i.nce; throu.... ... ..e
...c.... ...i.ions ... ... ... .cc. .ey are
..ouc..... ...l...l, ....n...o..e of ...t...ion.
I.... ... ...t..c.s ..o..all ...c..nce only ...ose
w...ch ...e non-s...tial; ou..r se..se ..s..c.s ...e ..tial
..rom ... ... l..in ...c...l.tions in co..r...e ex..r-
ience, ...ely, ou..r a..ea...ces in ...i.l. .t in.. r

133

possibility, or perception in general and its re-
l ... tinction or empirical determination is given, is not
to ... real knowledge ... knowledge
of the empirical in general, and has to be reckoned
... in ... tion of ... possibility ... and
every experience, which is certainly a transcendental
enquiry. 13'

## 122

### 3.  <u>Time and the Unity of Nature</u>

We have already drawn attention to the point that
in so far as a fundamental distinction between space and time
as extensive continua is made, there are two possibilities
as to how individuals may appear in these media.  We have
discussed these possibilities only with reference to the
category of substance, but we must now consider them in connection with those wider principles which bring about unity
in nature.  We must determine, moreover, how far this analysis
is  applicable to Kant's philosophy, and to what extent it
may be said that Kant's views represent that position which
we have called possibility B.  This necessarily involves a
decision as to whether time is more important than space in
the unity of nature which Kant proposes to explain.

It is commonly thought that Kant's philosophy represents an answer to Hume's scepticism, and in particular
to Hume's criticism of causality.  In the course of our investigation we attempt to show that Kant does, indeed,
formulate an answer to Hume, and that this answer depends
on the role of time in the unity of nature.

Possibility B is stated as follows:

There is a principle of individuation for time, and
this accounts for objects in space.

!ore explicitly, possibility B requires that principles which  overn the activities peculiar to the self, which are manifested by means of time-determinations, account for objects in space.  Just as laws which govern the movements of objects (substances) in space are thought, according to possibility A, to determine in general what kind of events will occur in the time-continuum, so according to possibility B, the rules which govern the activities of the self in relation to time must determine in general what kind of objects shall appear in space.  In both cases there must be both constitutive and regulative principles.  That is, not only must it be shown how events and objects,respectively, come to be, there must also be principles which indicate their natures and their relationships.

Now either of the positions can be given with imaginative connotations,- such as the conception of a self-existing substratum below or beyond the two media with their given differentiations,- or each can be reduced to the bare logical essentials which are necessary as principles or laws of the unification of nature, according to either possibility. It is with this latter contingency that we wish to deal. Since philosophers are ultimately all attempting to explain the same Nature, it is not surprising that the logical essentials of the two possibilities should show a marked

similarity.  There is, of course, room for much disagree-
ment concer. .ng those basic principles which are presupposed
by empirical laws of nature, and in this respect there is
room for dissimilarity between the two positions.  But in
so far as nature permits of quantitative determinations, the
category of quantity will be essential to both; and in so
far as nature exhibits enduring entities, some doctrine of
substance will be necessary.  Similarly, a recognition of
causation and quality would seem to be unavoidable.  These
are, perhaps, the most notable points on which there may be
agreement between the two positions, although even concerning
these, agreement may not be complete.  Considering, for
illustrative purposes, such principles as these to be examples
of common principles, then, the main difference between the
two positions will be that the one will  consider these
principles to be associated with matter and space, and the
other will consider them to be associated with the subject
and time.  But where material substance and the subject
are thought of simply as complexes of functions embodying
the necessary principles, the two positions will represent
a clear antithesis such as we have drawn between the two
possibilities.  Either one must explain events in time
through principles pertaining to space, or one must explain
objects in space through principles pertaining to time.

## 125

On epistemological questions, the two positions may
a ree or disa gree.  uither matter or the subject may be considered rationalistically so that the principles pertaining
to each may be conceived as necessary and apodeictic.  Alternatively, matter may be thought to exhibit only probable
laws, or the principles pertaining to the self nay be considered to be merel, probable, as for example, Hume's laws
of association.  The intrusion of epistemological questions,
however, reveals the close connection between the self and
time.  Hume's criticism of causation would have been impossible without his distinction between the future and the
past. That is, it would not have been possible for Hume to
maintain that the primary impression of the idea of necessary
connection derives from customary association if he had not
believed that human experience was ordered in time in such
a way that there were past repetitions which may or may not
be exemplified in future events.  Similarly, as we hope to
show, Kant's Copernican revolution would have been impossible
had he not shown that the principles pertaining to the knowing subject, which are constitutive of objects, have application to experience through time alone.

For Kant, the whole phenomenal world has reality
only in relation to the cognitive faculties of the self, or
the human mind.  But those cognitive faculties which produce
the order and unity of this phenomenal world are not

subjective  in the psychological sense.  Kant is not giving
us a genetic psychology.  In what sense, then, does the
phenomenal world have its character only in relation to the
knower?  The whole transcendental apparatus, including the
Transcendental Aesthetic, the categories, the Transcendental
Unity of Apperception, the Transcendental Imagination, is
not psychologically subjective, and does not issue from the
activities of a numerical plurality of human minds.  We
must be entitled to say in t is regard that if Kant's philosophy is true, it must have been true long before human
life ever arose on earth.  Granted that the phenomenal world
has reality only in relation to these transcendental conditions, in what sense are we entitled to call these conditions
subjective?  As Paton points out, the self in relation to
which the phenomenal world is real, (as appearance) is not
the phenomenal self.

> If the self which is known in inner sense is
> only phenomenal, what are we to say of the self which
> knows?  Is the knowing self a thing-in-itself, although
> the known self is only an appearance?  To this question
> Kant's answer is obscure; but perhaps we may say, in
> the light of his moral philosophy, that the self does
> belong to the realm of things-in-themselves, although
> as a thing-in-itself it can never be known by us.  135

If it be conceded that the self which knows must be
a thing-in-itself, on what basis do we distinguish one thing-
in-itself fro  another as subject and object?

## 127

> Above all, can we believe --if this is Kant's
> doctrine --that the world as we experience it is due
> to the interplay of two unknown thin s-in-themselves,
> one of which is a self, while the other is perhaps not
> a self?  It is difficult to accept one wholly unknown
> factor.  It is almost impossible to accept two.  If
> they are wholly unknown, how can they be distinguished
> from one another?    136

Even if we delate the thing-in-itself from Kant's
philosophy, and consider that his main point lies in his
discovery of the logical presuppositions of empirical knowledge, the difficulty remains.  If we strip Kant's terminology of its psychological connotations, the nature of the
difficulty becomes clearer.  A basic element in Kant's position lies in his view that universal and necessary proposi-
tional forms lie at the base of the unity of nature.  This
order of one nature is, we take it, quite independent of any
particular judgments made by human beings.  As Kant himself
often points out, the activities which make up the psychology
of any particular human being are just another part of the
phenomenal world, in so far as they are sensational.  Thus,
the subject-object distinction of psychology is quite irrelevant to the subject-object distinction which figures in the
Copernican revolution.  The knower in relation to which the
phenomenal world gets its order and unity is not the knower
qua psychological subject.  How, then, can this knower, as
a transcendental presupposition of empirical knowledge, be
distinguished from the ordering principles of an objective

world?  Kant's view seems to be that the intelligible, the
logical presuppositions of empirical knowledge pertain to
the activities of an ego or self, and yet his whole criticism
of rational psychology rests on the point that except for
its purely logical functions this ego is empty.

> That the 'I' of apperception, and therefore the
> 'I' in every act of thought, is <u>one</u>; and cannot be re-
> solved into a plurality of subjects, and consequently
> signifies a logically simple subject, is something al-
> ready contained in the very concept of thought, and is
> therefore an analytic proposition.  But this does not
> mean that the thinking 'I' is a simple <u>substance</u>.  137

It is evident that one reason at least for Kant's
association of the ordering principles of nature with an
ego or subject lies in his view that logic pertains to the
thinking activities of a subject, and in his doctrine of
<u>judgment</u>.  But if we approach the question from the point
of view of human knowledge, as Kant did, we discover a second set of reasons for making the subject-object distinction
at the transcendental level.  <u>A priori</u> knowledge is knowledge which can be had prior to experience, i.e. knowledge
which is independent of experience and which does not issue
from the senses.  Thus <u>a priori</u> knowledge is independent of
the passage of time.  Because the mind contributes the form
of possible experience, we can according to Kant, know something about future experience prior to our having it.  Kant,
indeed, does not limit his statement of the scope of <u>a priori</u>
knowledge to future experience, but extends it to all possible

experience. Nevertheless, his doctrine necessarily implies
that we can know something about future experience prior
to our experiencing it. A posteriori knowledge, on the other
hand, is knowledge which must await experience, and which
therefore depends on the passage of time. If our knowledge
conforms to objects, we can know nothing of objects prior
to what is revealed in experience with the passage of time.
We can know something about objects prior to experience only
if objects conform to our peculiar modes of cognition.

> If intuition must conform to the constitution
> of the objects, I do not see how we could know anything
> of the latter a priori; but if the object (as object
> of the senses) must conform to the constitution of our
> faculty of intuition, I have no difficulty in conceiving
> such a possibility. Since I cannot rest in these in-
> tuitions if they are to become known, but must relate
> them as representations to something as their object,
> and determine this latter through them, either I must
> assume that the concepts, by means of which I obtain
> this determination, conform to the object, or else I
> assume that the objects, or what is the same thing,
> that the experience in which alone, as given objects,
> they can be known, conform to the concepts. In the
> former case, I am again in the same perplexity as to
> how I can know anything a priori in regard to the ob-
> jects. In the latter case the outlook is more hopeful. 138

This is Kant's statement of what is involved in the
Copernican revolution. There are three points necessary
for its success: (a) Kant must show that there are pure
concepts which may be constitutive and regulative of our
knowledge of objects; (b) he must show that these categories do necessarily apply to objects of knowledge, or to
put it otherwise, he must show that if we are to have any

wledge of objects of experience at all, we must think
m by means of the categories; (c) we must show that ex-
ience is, in fact, constituted in such a fashion that
categories are constitutive and regulative of it.  In
er to make clear what we mean by (c), perhaps it would
better to speak of the phenomenal world instead of ex-
ience.  For this third requirement does not concern a
etic psychological explanation, a thing quite foreign
Kant's purposes, but concerns how the categories are, in
t, constitutive and regulative of objects in the phenome-
world.  Without the fulfilment of this third requirement,
t's Copernican revolution is incomplete.  Kant has himself
arly acknowledged the necessity of these three require-
ts.

In the metaphysical deduction the a priori origin
of the categories has been proved through their complete
agreement with the general logical functions of thought;
in the transcendental deduction we have shown their
possibility as a priori modes of knowledge of objects
of an intuition in general.  We have now to explain the
possibility of knowing a priori by means of categories,
whatever objects may present themselves to our senses,
not indeed in respect of the form of their intuition,
but in respect of the laws of their combination, and so,
as it were, of prescribing laws to nature, and even of
making nature possible.  For unless the categories dis-
charged this function, there could be no explaining
why everything that can be presented to our senses must
be subject to laws which have their origin a priori in
the understanding alone.  139

Our chief interest in this third requirement, the

second Edition of the _Critique_, lies in the point that the
"combination" of which  ant speaks  ust take place in accordance with cate ories scher atised by means of ti e-determinations alone.  For we could never know anything prior to experience if the passage of time itself did not embody those
very principles which are said to contribute the form of
possible experience.  If the passage of ti e  ent on independently of these principles, we should never be entitled
to suppose that the future will rese ble the past, or that
future experience will have any of the characteristics of
past experience.  Although the principles the selves are
independent of time, they must be constitutive and regulative of objects of experience through time, and _only_ _through_
_time_; otherwise there would be no necessary reason for
supposing that these logical principles, rules of synthesis,
were constitutive of future experience.  It is just this
requirement which must be met if  ume's statement that "the
supposition _that_ _the_ _future_ _rese bles_ _the_ _past_, is not
founded on arguments of any kind, but is deriv'd entirely
from habit" 140 is to be refuted.

Thus, if  ant is to be considered as giving a conclusive ans er to Hume, he must sho  that contrary to  ume's
contentions, we have reason to believe that the future will
resemble the past.  T' is can be shown not merely by exhibiting
the principles constitutive of objects of knowledge for

intuition in general, but by showing that the passage of
time, which allo  c  ti  ous increase of sensible intuitions, co bines t'ese inti itions in accordance with the
principles constitutive of objects.  In ot er words time
itself ust bring about the existence of objects of future
experience.  T'e first part of Lant's Transcendental Deduction does not suffice to prove that this will be the case,
as Paton observes.

> To put the matter in another way--it might be
> a mere accident whether appearances conformed to the
> cate ories or not.  No doubt if they did not conform,
> we should cease to have experience; but in that case
> so much the worse for us.  So far as the argument has
> gone at present, the conformity of appearances to the
> cate ories  ust indeed have occurred; for there has
> been suc  a thing as human experience.  That conformity
> might, however, have been due to a pre-established
> harmony arran ed by the beneficence of God; and any
> view of this type is emphatically rejected by Lant. 141

We  ight show conclusively that we can know of objects only those which conform to our peculiar  odes of cognition, but this does not b, itself in the least show that
we shall ever in the future  eet wit  such objects.  The
statement that either knowledge confor c to objects, or
objects must conform to our vays of knowing objects, and
the defense of the latter alternativ , does not refute
Hume's position.  Even though objects must conform to our
knowledge, we are not entitled to assume that future experience will exhi it objects  ' ic' conform to our knowledge,
unless time itself and its irreversible passage <u>is shown to</u>

brin_ such object  i _o existe.ce.   e mi_ht cease to have
experi_ ce in ! nt's  _ase of t e _crm, i._. as e pirical
_nowled e.  _it is th t not just H  e's point, n mely, that
human experie_c  do_s not necessarily re_resent e _irical
knowled e, sinc_ t ere is no proof tl at the future will
resemble the past?  Thus, if I'ume is to be effectively answered, the _ _priori_ principles constitutive of objects
must  anifest themselves by means of ti e-determinations,
and not through s-atial determinations.  This is, we feel,
a reasonable explan tion of why Kant has schematised the
categories by  e_ns of time-determinations alone.

  There are, however, other reasons for this conclusion.  Some weight must perhaps be _iven to the fact that
Kant had ample opportunity to repair his oversight in omit-
ting space from the Transcendental schematism, if, indeed,
it re_resents an oversight on his part.  He could, if he
had desired, have included spatial schemata in the second
edition of the _Critique_.  But he did not avail himself of
this opportunity.   e must conclude, then, that either his
acumen failed, or that his philosophy did not necessitate
spatial sc'e._ta.  Even if Kant was not prepared to _raft
a len_thy ex_lanation of these schemata, he could easily
have included a foot-note indicating that later workers in
the new science mi_ht appropriately fill in the lacuna.

## 134

For Kant, time cannot be said to be an ultimate
reality.  It is not a thing-in-itself.  Yet time, as a determining condition throughout the phenomenal world is all-
pervasive.  It is through time alone that the categories
become schematised, and hence are able to determine the
character of appearances.

> We thus find that the schema of each category
> contains and makes capable of representation only a
> determination of time.  142

The principles which represent the rules under which
the existence of all appearances is ordered are all deter-
inations of time, and time alone.

> The principles can therefore have no other pur-
> pose save that of being the conditions of the unity of
> <u>empirical</u> knowledge in the synthesis of appearances.
> But such unity can be thought only in the <u>schema</u> of the
> pure concept of the understanding.  143

The unity of empirical knowledge is a result of the
function of the original synthetic unity of apperception,
and it is this that is the condition of the regulative and
constitutive principles.  Without this synthetic unity of
apperception there could be no unity of experience at all.
But this unity is manifested in principles which express
only time-determinations.

> In this third [medium], the essential form of
> which consists in the synthetic unity of the apper-
> ception of all appearances, we have found <u>a priori</u>
> conditions of complete and necessary determination of
> time for all existence in the [field of] appearance,
> without which even empirical determination of time
> would be impossible.  144

intain the essential requirement of possibility B,
y, that principles or rules which bring about the unity
ture apply directly to time itself and not to space.

indeed, is not given whole as the determinable in which
experience finds a position. Every appearance is de-
ned in its position in time because the categories
directly to time.

That determines for each appearance its position
in time is the rule of the understanding through which
alone the existence of appearances can acquire synthetic
unity as regards relations of time; and that rule consequently determines the position (in a manner that is)
a priori valid for each and every time.  145

Also, Kant gives the clearest possible expression
e other main requirement of possibility B, namely,
everything else in nature is determined by time, and
he other way around as would be the case according to
bility A. All increase in empirical knowledge, or ex-
nce, Kant tells us, is nothing but an advance in time.
ollowing this statement is a most important assertion
ich Kant says, without qualification, that "This ad-
in time determines everything, and is not itself

in connection with givi   a  effective a s or to "u.e,

n ely, t'at a priori principles constit tive of objects

 ust manif st tl e..elves by  e ns of  i e-deter ir ations.

It is just .ant's poi  t  t future experi nce must have

a priori features because the a vance of ti e itself guaran-

tees it.

> In the sa e  anner, t'erefore, in which time
> contains the sensible a priori condition of the possi-
> bility of   conti uous advance of the existing to
> what follows, the understanding, by virtue of the
> unity of ap erception, is the a priori condition of
> the possibility of a continuous determination of all
> positions for the appeara ces in this time. . . 147

It is true that  ere .ant is referring principally

to causation, but it is clear that all of the other categories

must likewise be determinative of objects through ti e alone.

For if they were not, the certainty of our a priori knowledge

in respect of the  would still be endangered by Hume's inex-

orable clai  that we h ve no proof that the future vill re-

se ble the past.  Eve  thoug  ve  ig t be certain that every

future experience vill be causally leter ined, ve  ould not

be entitled to assu e that it wo ld h ve  ny other  rriori

features.   ant  ust tl erefore show that all of the catego-

ries have  p lic.tion to ex erience by  eans of ti e-deter-

minations.  I' is is, in f ct, .hat he doe., and so we can

say that his ans er to  u e is co plete.

 ant held t' t n ture was a dyna ical whole rather

than a purely  ec'unical one.   e was suspicious of the

concept of a void, or empty space and sought to show, in the _Critique_ _of_ _Pure_ _Reason_ and in the _Metaphysical_ _Foundations_ _of_ _Natural_ _Science_ that the concept of empty space was unnecessary for physical science. For this reason alone we can say that Kant definitely rejects possibility A, in which the givenness of all space either as a relational complex or an absolute container is an essential point. Although the spatial aspect of appearances is not by any means ignored in the adumbration of the Analytic of Principles, Kant expresses these principles in terms of determinations of time.

> The concept of magnitude in general can never be explained except by saying that it is that determination of a thing whereby we are enabled to think how many times a unit is posited in it. But this how-many-times is based on successive repetition, and therefore on time and the synthesis of the homogeneous in time. Reality, in contradistinction to negation, can be explained only if we think time (as containing all being) as either filled with being or as empty. If I leave out permanence (which is existence in all time), nothing remains in the concept of substance save only the logical representation of a subject . . 148

Only the three Postulates of Empirical Thought are elaborated without specific stress on time, although these three postulates are so defined as to presuppose the other principles which _are_ stated in terms of time-determinations. In any case, as Kant remarks, "The principles of modality are not, however, objectively synthetic". They add nothing to the order in time-relations of the objective existence

itself.  The Analogies of Experience, for example, are "Prin
ciples of the determination of the existence of appearances
in time, according to all its three modes, viz., the relatio
of time to itself as a magnitude (the magnitude of existence
that is, duration), the relation in time as a successive
series, and finally the relation in time as a sum of all
simultaneous existence".  Similarly, even though the Axioms
of Intuition and the Anticipations of Perception are mathematical rather than dynamical principles, that is, they are
necessary formal conditions of experience pertaining to
"the mere intuition of an appearance in general",  rather
than with the dynamical, on-going progress of nature as it
exists, they are nonetheless all dependent on time.  This
requires further comment.

One concept which is involved in the Axioms of Intuition and the Anticipations of Perception is quantity or
magnitude, the schema of which is number, which is "simply
the unity of the synthesis of the manifold of a homogeneous
intuition in general, a unity due to my generating time

itself in the apprehension of the intuition".[152] Kant consistently tells us that magnitude comes about by means of a successive synthesis of part to part.  ithout this successive synthesis, we get no determinate intuition.

> Inner sense, on the other hand, contains the mere form of intuition, but without combination of the manifold in it, and therefore so far contains no <u>determinate</u> intuition, which is possible only through the consciousness of the determination of the manifold by the transcendental act of imagination (synthetic influence of the understanding upon inner sense), which I have entitled figurative synthesis. [153]

In support of this statement Kant draws attention to the fact that in order to conceive of a magnitude, we must construct it in thought, by a successive synthesis.

> This we can always perceive in ourselves. We cannot think a line without <u>drawing</u> it in thought, or a circle without describing it. [154]

Kant holds that this is true not only of geometry but also of numbers, for, indeed, the schema of quantity <u>is</u> number.

> Thus our counting, as is easily seen in the case of larger numbers, is a synthesis according to concepts, because it is executed according to a common ground of unity, as, for instance, the decade. In terms of this concept, the unity of the synthesis of the manifold is rendered necessary. [155]

It is clear that space and time, or rather the spatial and temporal aspects of the phenomenal world, have magnitude only because of the successive synthesis due to the transcendental imagination. This is why, according to Kant, space and time are continuous magnitudes. In a passage

of unusual clarity, Kant explains how determinate magnitudes
of space and ti e are  enerated.

> Such  a nitudes may also be called <u>flowing</u>,
> since the synthesis of productive ima ination involved
> in their production is a progression in ti e, and the
> continuity of time is ordinarily desi nated by the
> term flowing or flowing away.   156

This reveals, as well, a point of comparison with
Bergson, namely, that continuity does not stem from the intellect itself, but is a property of time.  e shall discuss
this point later on.  What is important here, however, is
that quantity of anything in nature in general, is the result of a successive synthesis in time.  Thus the principle
of the Axioms of Intuition, namely, that all intuitions are
extensive magnitudes, does not depend on space itself, or
the application of the concept of quantity to space, but
depends on a successive synthesis in time, which is the means
whereby all quanta arise.  Kant's doctrine seems to be that
the successive transcendental synthesis by means of time-
determinations, that is, by means of the schema of quantity,
brings determinate spaces into existence.  Prior to this
synthesis there are no objects.  Objects are not spatial
except in so far as spatial magnitude is generated by means
of the successive advance of time.  That is, as time itself
is extended by successive addition of part to part, space
is also generated <u>in the same synthesis</u>, as a determinate
quantum.  For this reason, no doubt, Kant can say that as

forms of intuition neither space nor time are objects.

> The mere form of intuition, without substance,
> is in itself no object, but the merely formal condition
> of an object (as appearance), as pure space and time
> (ens imaginarium). These are indeed something, as forms
> of intuition, but are not themselves objects which
> are intuited.   157

As we have seen, outer sense is an abstract aspect of inner sense. What is in space is _ipso facto_ in time. Thus, we can say that in that area of appearances which are in both space and time, the transcendental synthesis productive of these appearances is a successive synthesis of both space and time, productive of determinate magnitudes of space during a determinate length of time. This parallel growth of spatial and temporal determination seems naturally to suggest that it is necessary for Kant to say that the determining principles must apply to both space and time. But this is not only unnecessary; it would be of no use to Kant in carrying out the essential tasks of his Copernican revolution.

This is a corollary of what we have said about Kant's answer to Hume. Let us suppose that there are spatial schemata of the categories which enter into the constitution of objects of experience, guaranteeing that objects shall _by that means_ have certain general _a priori_ features. By what right are we entitled to suppose that such spatially extended objects will ever be present to us in experience?

f the sp tial features of objects v re nisured by that
eans, we would not nec ssarily have synt etic _a priori_
knowledge about the spatial constitution of future experience (in the Humean r ther than the Kantian sense), because
we would have no guarantee that future exp rience would reveal such objects.  Future experience might, for all we know,
reveal the utter emptiness of such knowledge.  It is undoubtedly hard to imagine such a contingency, but our subjective
inability to imagine it, does not, in itself, constitute a
conclusive argument that the future will rese ble the past.
For this reason, spatial schemata would, so to speak, be a
fifth wheel in Kant's system.  Hume's very point is that
psychologically we have become accustomed to certain regular
features of experience, and for that reason we expect a repetition of them in the future, and Hume shows conclusively,
if he shows anything, that this psychological conditioning
gives us no certainty whatever about future experience.
And once this point is admitted, we may say that as a matter
of fact objects do have spatial features, but that is far
from guaranteeing that they _must_ have them.  Thus, just as
Hume's arguments rest on the fundamental distinction between the future and that past, so likewise, Kant's arguments that objects of experience must have certain _a priori_
spatial features must rest on the view that the passage of
time will bring such objects of experience into existence.

...nd for this ...urpose s...tial sc'...cm... t... are unsuit...ble, for
we must rec'on with tl e possibility t' t ... spatial features
of o...jects are ...rel... ...cci ...its of ... ...rticular time.    ...ant,
himself, rec'ons ...ith thi... po...sibility, for although he argues that we c n never in prin...ci l... represe ...t to ourselves
the absence of space, "we c...n quite well t...nk it as empty
of objects". [158]   That there are objects _in_ space, and hence
having certain spatial features, must depend, then, on time-
determinations.   ...hus, it is only because ...a ...nitude, according to Kant, is always the result of a categorical determination of ti...e, that space itself can have ma...nitude.

> I cannot represent to myself a line, however
> small, without drawing it in thought, that is genera-
> ting from a point all its parts one after another. [159]

> The mathematics of space (geometry) is based
> upon this successive synthesis of the productive ima-
> gination in the generation of figures. [160]

The Axioms of Intuition do not, therefore, we maintain imply spatial schemata, but quite the reverse.   It is
just because the spatial features of objects _do not_ depend
on the direct spatial schematism of the concept of quantity,
that we can say _a priori_ of experience i...1 general (including
future experience) that objects of experience must in their
intuition, be extensive magnitudes.

This implies, however, an intimate connection between
space and ti...e, t'...e two fundamentally distinct forms of intuition, such that if a c...rtain quantum of ti...e is generated,

a certain quantum of space will by this process also be
generated.  If our analysis of the meanings of inner an
outer sense is correct, however, this automatically fol
For if outer sense is an abstract aspect of inner sense
the wide meaning, then, if time is gen. ated in that ar
of sensibility which has a spatial aspect, a determinat
magnitude of space must also be generated, just because
outer sense is only an abstraction from inner sense.  B
this implies some kind of union of space and time, and
the standpoint of the understanding this is a perplexin
thing.

Here we must recall what we have said in Chapte
Two, Section One, about the difficulties of cognizing t
relatedness of space and time if they are two unique pa
ticulars.  Strictly speaking, we cannot <u>understand</u> this
union, for if they are essentially unlike, there is nothing in common between them.  For this reason we have
that in thinking about inner and outer sense, the empha
must be placed on <u>sense</u>.  We can never explain by means
concepts how it is that an advance of time can generate
magnitude of space, any more than we can explain becomi
in general.  For this reason, we take it, Kant very pro
does not attempt to explain it, but refers to our acqua
tance with this union, in effect, by saying of the tran
dental synthesis,  "this we can always perceive in ours

notion, however, considered as the describing
of a space, is a pure act of the successive synthesis
of the manifold in outer intuition in general by means
of the productive imagination. . .162

For Kant, only time is intrinsically successive, or
1. Space, in itself, is an aggregate not a series.
tells us, furthermore, how we happen to have the con-
of succession. We derive it from time itself, as the
of inner sense, and the 'motion' of synthesis in time.

notion, as an act of the subject. . .and therefore the synthesis of the manifold in space, first
produces the concept of succession --if we abstract
from this manifold and attend solely to the act through
which we determine the inner sense according to its
form.    163

Unless we are prepared to reject these statements
f hand, we must admit that Kant is here attempting to
in not becoming itself, but the manner in which the
ories apply, as principles, to the passage of time
f, and hence how time brings into existence determinate
a of space. It must be added, of course, that Kant
attempts to specify only in general the a priori spa-
features of objects. He does not try to tell us why
ticular thing is round or square, etc., a matter which,

have a priori knowledge of such a specific character.  But
it seems clear that this general feature which we can know
a priori about objects of experience, depends basically on
the fact that the categories, by means of schemata expressed
as time-determinations, apply directly and solely to time
itself, the form of inner sensibility.

> The understanding does not, therefore, find in
> inner sense such a combination of the manifold, but
> produces it, in that it affects that sense.    164

> We have also proved that the only manner in
> which objects can be given to us is by modification
> of our sensibility; and finally, that pure a priori
> concepts, in addition to the function of understanding
> expressed in the category, must contain a priori cer-
> tain formal conditions of sensibility, namely, those
> of inner sense.    165

> On the other hand, the schema of a pure concept
> of understanding can never be brought into any image
> whatsoever.  It is simply the pure synthesis, determined
> by a rule of that unity, in accordance with concepts,
> to which the category gives expression.  It is a tran-
> scendental product of imagination, a product which con-
> cerns the determination of inner sense in general ac-
> cording to conditions of its form (time), in respect
> of all representations, so far as these representations
> are to be connected a priori in one concept in con-
> formity with the unity of apperception.    166

The unity and consistency of Kant's thought is truly
remarkable, for he does not in any essential respects de-
part from his view that the order of Nature is the result
of the categorical determination of time.  Even the a priori
spatial features of objects depend on it.  Time and the principles relating to it are logically prior to the spatial

as ect of the  leno e  l  orl . 'ince it    'ume who
awakened Kant fro  his "o matic slumbers", we  ay conclude
that K·nt tool p·rticular  ains to ensure that <u>all</u> synthetic
a  riori knowle  e, (includin  tl t relatin  to the <u>a priori</u>
spatial features of objects), should esc   'ume's destruc-
tive criticis. , his rel ntless dictum that  e have no reason
to believe that the future will resemble the past.

Not only are tr nscendental sche ata for space un-
necess·ry and redundant for Kant's pur oses, the acceptance
of the  would create grave problems relating to other parts
of Kant's system.  The inclusion of space in the schematism,
and according it an equal status with time in the formulation
of the principles which ensure the unity and order of Nature,
167
tempts one, as Paton points out,    to regard the mind itself
as spatial.  It mi ht be more accurate in this re ard to say
that if the categories were schematised in space as well as
time, this would tend to obliterate the distinction between
inner and outer sense on which so much of Kant's doctrine
rests.  We assume that it was Kant's purpose to explain the
<u>a  riori</u> principles governing <u>one</u>  ature.  If it is true
that the princi les which ensure that there shall be one
Nature must do so by functioning through the media of both
space and time together, then the logical result would seem
to be that the sphere of application of space must be absolutely coextensive with the sphere of a plic tion of time.

How could there be unity in the functioning of these principles, which, according to this view, require both space
and time for their expression, if they apply to an area of
appearances which are in time alone? For if the categories
must be expressed in spatial determinations as well as
time-determinations in order that there should be a unity
in Nature, it follows that they do not function separately
in their separate media, but function in unison in space
and time.  The whole phenomenal world, including phenomenal selves, must, if it is to be one unified nature, be
everywhere spatio-temporal.  For if the categories are the
ground of all determination of appearances as phenomena,
then their schematism through both forms of sensibility
will mean that <u>all</u> appearances will be determined both in
space and time.  In this case, it will be necessary to deny
that the mind is non-spatial.

Mental activities, of course, need not be considered to be in space, since they are not appearances.  But
mental activities, or psychological events, would have to
be explained as being, nothing more nor less than events
in the phenomenal world.  It would have to be held that
they were in principle amenable to a <u>physical</u> explanation
in the same manner as any other events in the phenomenal
world.  This would be to take the approach of that theory
which we have called possibility A, for in the one Nature

which is co.plet ly s. ti -te poral  only possible events
i time are thos which  rhod' t e .ve nts, (changes
of place) of objects in  ce. Eve.t'oug' it c 'e said,
on this view, t'at  t.l activities re 1 t e alone, the
point is that they re 'n ti e alore .n t'e s e sense, and
only bec use, all events .r in ti e. There is thus no distinguishing between mental events a  a iy other 'inds of
events. They all occur in o c patio-temporal nature. From
this follows the inevitable result that  a terialistic
psychology must be formulated, one moreover, w ich would
explain all aspects of mental activities, including logical
thinking. and this is a thing which I at ex licitly repudiates.

> For  perception is so t'ing real, and its
> simplicity is already iven in the mere fact of its
> possibility. Now in space t'ere is not'ing real which
> can be si ple; points which are the only simple things
> in space, are m rely limits, not t'e selves anything
> that can as parts serve to constitute space. From this
> follows the i possi'ility of any explanation in _materi-
> alist_ terms of the constitution of the self as a merely
> thin in s 'ject.   168

Kant's idealism is not to be insaid, even though
it figures in his syste merely as the bare logical functions of the mind. This is why we have devoted some discussion to pointing out th t the reason why Kant regarded
the unifying principles of Nature to ste from the subject,
rather than as being the ordering principles of an objective world, rests, at least in part in his doctrine of

jud ment.  he inuependent origin of the cate ories, themselves, in the nature of human thought would be quite inexplicable in terms of a materialistic psycholog .  e
cannot avoid this difficulty simply by fallin_ back on
their purely lo_ic_l nature, for lo_ic itself must have
been discovered by human minds, and logical thinking must
always involve mental activities which take place in time.
But how can the forms of judgment ori_inate in objects?

There is a further awkward result associated with
the view that the categories must be schematised by means
of spatial deter inations, and this stems from Kant's
fundamental distinction between space and time.  We assume
that Kant must have thought that space and time were ultimately separate and distinct, or he would never have distinguished them as two different for_s of sensibility.
The synthetic <u>a</u> <u>priori</u> knowledge which Kant believes is
possessed in p ysics concerns, above all, the relations
among phenomena.  The Analogies, taken together, declare
that all appearances must lie in one nature, and this is
because the transcendental unity of apperception imposes
this unity on all appearances through <u>one</u> <u>kind</u> <u>of</u> <u>relation</u>
<u>only</u>, <u>namely</u>, <u>the</u> <u>time-relation</u>.  If this unity is i posed
on two different forms of sensibility, then on principle
there seems to be no reason why there would not be two
unified natures of phenomena determined in space and time

respectively.  The simplest, if perhaps the roughest way,
to put this point would be to say that if the schemata give
the categories meaning, and if there are two schemata, one
spatial and another temporal, for each category, and if,
further, there is a fundamental distinction between space
and time, then each category will have two separate and
distinct meanings.  There will thus be two natures.

Kant's motives in schematising the categories by
means of time-determinations display several aspects, and
these are all connected with his fundamental distinction
between space and time:  (a) logical functions stem from
the mind, or the subject; (b) the mental activities, including logical thinking, of human subjects are in time
alone; (c) a materialistic psychology is impossible; (d) a
complete justification of synthetic a priori knowledge,
even that relating to the spatial features of objects, can
be carried out by means of categorical determinations of
time alone; (e) for this justification, spatial schemata
are not only not needed, but they could not possibly serve
the purpose.  Thus, in general, there are two basic reasons
for Kant's making a fundamental distinction between space
and time, for considering time to be logically prior to
space, and for giving time a position of overwhelming importance in the unification of nature.  These are, first,
the indispensable and irreducible idealistic element in

'ant's yste would other ise h ve been jeop rdized. The
very lynch-pins of ant's thou 't, n ely, the transcendental unity of pperc ption, nd the indepen it ori in of
the c te ories in the n ture of lo ic l thi ing, would
have been difficult, if not i ossible, to mai tain. pper-
ception and lo ical thi ing pertain to t e s bject, and
in terms of human psychology, it is only t e fact that these
mental activities are in ti o alone and not lso in space
that distin uishes them from events in the spatio-te poral
phenomenal world. Only some quasi-miraculous doctrine of
emer ence could locate the in an exclusively spatio-temporal
Nature. ant, t least, ives no indiction that he was
tending in t is direction. For hi, lo ic and its peculiar
norms are a posse sion of the ind in ependent of the world
of phyical objects, in the sense that k owled o of them
is not be explained by means of the motions of bodies. If
they were not in nendent, it is extremely difficult to
see how I ant could hold that forms of judgment are prior
to n constitutive of such objects. nd even s p eromenal
selves, we must be ble to be conscious of the forms of
jud ment, psyc ologically, that is, e must have been able
to discover them, nd be co scious of our lo ical thinking
by means of ent l ctivities. The mental activities of
the phe om al self must therefore be separated clearly
from events in t e external world. ant's distinction

between inner and outer sense, which rests, at bottom, on
his fundamental distinction between space and time, is, we
maintain, the chief means whereby he acco lishes this important separation.

e find, therefore, that it is very misleading to
speak of  ant's view as a "metaphysics of experience". The
expression is correct enough as far s it goes, in that it
does imply what Kant's chief metaphysical interest was.
But it also seems to su est an omission of the independent,
idealistic source of the principles constitutive of experience.  For Kant's philosophy is not primarily a metaphysics
of experience, but rather a metaphysics of logic.  The fundamental metaphysical fact, for Kant, is the primacy of
judgment.

The second basic reason for the importance of time
in Kant's philosophy, and for the consequent derivative role
of space, relates to the effectiveness of Kant's answer to
Hume.  Since we have already discussed this at length, we
need not linger further over it here.  We must take the opportunity at this point, however, to remark that had Kant
not made a fundamental distinction between space and time,-
had he obliterated all distinction between space and time,-
he would never have been able to rebut Hume's criticism at
all.  For Hume's main argument can be stated equally in

terms of diver e r i s of space-ti e,  s it can be in terms
of t e diffe  c et n t e fut r  n t  past, as lon
 s it is        r 'oxic ll eno ', t' t  identical
elf can b at  fer t re ions of space-ti e.   ant's answer d per  o t'e vi  th t the c te ories co dition the
tem or l s ce ssiv ess of  e tr  ce ental synthesis of
ina ination.  ut if the univ rse is laid out co pletely
in an ete  l fo r- ine sional  ifold, t' ere can be no
question o s cc  siv ess, nd hence no synt  sis t all,
at least in I a t's se se of the term.  In a dition, accordin  to   ifold theor  i  ich th ore is no dis inction
betwe  sp cc and ti e, i ividu ls  come  m tter of co -
vention.  It is  rd to see l ow t ere could be any but an
arbit ry  o er i nature, if thi  s can " ove bac  and
forth in ti e",  ependi   on  ou  e choo e to re ard them.
T ere ce tai ly co ld be  nccssary lo ical order.  A
develop  c o I  is's vie  in t is irection  uld seem to
be extre ely  n- a tian.  On the ot' er  nd, the physical
theory of sp ce-ti  sce s to retai an intrinsic difference
betuoen sp ce  nd timo, a dist nction hich is involved in
the refer nce to the obs rvation of notion.  ime is dis-
tinguis d fro s ace by its s ccessiven ss to the conscious
ind.  And this, of course, is the very basis of I ant's
distinction.  In t is respect at least, the hysical theory
of space-time does not seem to be inco patible with ant's

views. In so far as the physical theory of space-time presupposes a metaphysics similar to possibility 1, however, it would be opposed to a metaphysics of space and time. But this opposition might possibly be removed by a proper distinction between measured time and primordial time, i.e. becoming.

Kant's metaphysics is, if not much else, a unified and amazingly consistent body of doctrine. His view of the transcendental conditions of human experience, his recognition of the role of logic and apperception, necessitate a distinction between space and time such that the subject, _qua_ phenomenal self, is distinguished from the material world and objects in space, in that the self is in time alone. We can express this by saying that, for Kant, part of the distinction between subject and object consists in the fact that the inner activities of the self are in time alone. Kant makes use of this point and the consequent flux of inner sense in his proof of the emptiness of rational psychology. Thus, in Kant's view, human mental activities have a very close association with time, a topic which we must now discuss.

[illegible]
[illegible]

### 1.  Time and Inner Experience

Having clarified sufficiently for our purpose the
role of space and time in Kant's philosophy, we are now in
a position to introduce Bergson's views, and to compare them
with those of Kant.  We have already seen that Kant's views
necessarily involve the point that the self is in time only.
We must now explore the significance of this intimate relation between the self and time.  We shall present evidence
that Bergson's philosophy parallels that of Kant in several
important respects, namely, in holding that the inner
experience of the self allows a direct apprehension of the
reality of time and change, that this inner experience is
not explicable in terms of science appropriate to outer
sense, that the concept of the self is empty except in so
far as it is conceived as a logical function, and that in
several essential ways Bergson's distinction between inner
and outer sense resembles that of Kant.

Kant and Bergson agree on a point of fundamental
importance, namely, that the empirical self is characterized
by a perpetual flux.  In so far as we are conscious of
ourselves and our inner state, we are conscious of a

continuous chan e.  For Lant, when we empirically attend

to that area of appearances called inner sense, (in the

narrow meanin ), our pri ary intuition is of this change.

> Consciousness of self according to deter-
> minations of our state in inner perception is merely
> empirical and always changing.  No fixed and abiding
> self can present itself in this flux of inner
> appearances.    170

Bergson makes the same point in more concrete,

figurative language:

> The existence of which we are most assured
> and which we know best is unquestionably our own,
> for of every other object we have notions which may
> be considered external and superficial, whereas, of
> ourselves our perception is internal and profound.
> What, then, do we find?. . .
> I find, first of all, that I pass from state
> to state.  I am warm or cold, I am merry or sad, I
> work or I do nothing, I look at what is around me or
> I think of something else.  Sensations, feelings,
> volitions, ideas-- such are the changes into which
> my existence is divided and which color it in turns.
> I chan e, then, without ceasing.  But this is not
> saying enough.  Change is far more radical than we
> are at first inclined to suppose.    171

Bergson, of course, reveals here the importance he

attaches to this intuition of change, in suggesting that

it is more radical than one might suppose.  While Kant

does not attach the same _kind_ of importance to this matter

that Bergson does, it is nevertheless an indispensable

element in his philosophy, opening up as it were, the

avenue through which Kant approaches _time_.  For, as we have

already emphasized, time is the form of inner sensibility

in the narrow meaning as well as in the wide meaning.

## 158

In addition, we must draw attention here to the similarity
of Bergson's point that our perception of ourselves is internal and profound, while our perception of objects is
external and superficial, to some of Kant's statements.
Kant tells us that "All that we know in matter is merely
relations (what we call the inner determinations of it are
inward only in a comparative sense)". [172]  Since Kant also
remarks that "we know of no determinations which are absolutely inner except those (given) through our inner sense", [173]
we may conclude that, for him, the primary meaning of the
term "inner" is derived from inner perception of ourselves.
This point, in fact, constitutes one of his main weapons
in his attack on Leibniz.  We do not know the inner nature
of anything except that of our phenomenal selves.  But
Kant quite clearly distinguishes this inner nature from
the determinations of external objects.

> But that which is inner in the state of a
> substance cannot consist in place, shape, contact or
> motion (these determinations being all outer rela-
> tions), and we can therefore assign to substance no
> inner state save that through which we ourselves
> inwardly determine our sense, namely, the state of
> representations.  174

One of the first questions which occurs concerning
this self-consciousness or perception of the self, as revealing a constant state of flux, is as to what meaning the
term "self" can have in this context.  Kant distinguishes
between inner sense or empirical apperception, which is in

constant flux, and the _faculty_ of apperception, and tells
us that "we intuit ourselves only as we are inwardly
affected".[175] The problem of how that which is in constant
flux can be determined in any way, we shall consider later.
For the present, we note only that one's inability to find
a suitable term, which at once indicates something determinate enough to be an object of knowledge, and at the same
time does not destroy the primary fact of the flux, is
revealing. What is uncovered in this inner intuition is,
so to speak, so slippery and transitory, that to apply
substantive terms to it seems to be a mistake. At any
rate the answers which Kant and Bergson give to this question are forthright and strikingly similar. There can be
little meaning for them in the notion of a permanent ego
or self in the flux of inner experience.

> But, as our attention has distinguished them
> and separated them artificially, it is obliged next
> to reunite them by an artifical bond. It imagines,
> therefore, a formless _ego_, indifferent and unchange-
> able, on which it threads the psychic states which
> it has set up as independent entities. Instead of a
> flux of fleeting shades merging into each other, it
> perceives distinct, and so to speak, _solid_ colors
> set side by side like the beads of a necklace; it
> must perforce then suppose a thread, also itself
> solid to hold the beads together. But if this color-
> less substratum is perpetually colored by that which
> colors it, it is for us, in its indeterminateness,
> as if it did not exist. . . [176]

We see here, in Bergson's words, something of the
Kantian doctrine of the indeterminateness of things-in-

themselves.  Indeed, for Kant, the emptiness of the concept
of the soul  is one of the char es he brin s a ainst rational
psychology, and the effectiveness of this charge rests on
Kant's view that inner experience reveals a constant flux.

> For in what we entitle 'soul', everything is
> in continual flux and there is nothing abiding except
> (if we must so express ourselves) the 'I' which is
> simple solely because its representation has no
> content.   177

It would be incorrect to call this inner intuition
itself time, for as Kant often remarks, "time itself cannot
be perceived".   178   Nevertheless, Kant holds that the nature
of time, the continuity of which "is ordinarily desi nated
by the term flowing or flowing away",   179   is the determinate
form "in which alone the intuition of inner states is possible".   180   While we cannot be said to perceive time, or to
have a knowledge of it by means of a concept, ("Time is
not a discursive, or what is called a general concept"),   181
we are nevertheless conscious of it as the peculiar form
in which this inner intuition takes place.  As such, we
can never be conscious of time as an object, especially as
a thing-in-itself.  We have the sense of time, however,
and recognize it as absolutely different from the sense
of space, although the way in which we can be said to have
these must be carefully specified to avoid misunderstanding
of Kant's doctrine.  We have a sense of time and a sense of
space, not as objects, or even as sensations; what we

actually sense are appe rances, so that we have the sense
of time and the sense of space, _only_ in so far as we recognize certain kinds of appearances as differently related,
i.e., as in time and as in space.  e have no sense of these
relations apart from the appearances which they relate, yet
we can in one way be said to have the sense of time and the
sense of space, in that we _do_ recognize appearances as differently related, some in time alone, ("the empirical object, which is called. . .an _inner_ object if it is represented only _in its time-relations_"),[182] others in both space and
time, "the conditions of sensible intuition, which carry
with them their own differences".[183]

Granted that the self as it appears to inner sense,
in the narrow meaning, is not time itself, but is _in_ time,
and taking Kant's words at their face value, that this self
is in constant flux, it is now necessary to enquire into
the character of the flux itself, and to determine how Kant
thought of it.  It will be helpful in this regard to introduce his views on psychology and what kind of a science it
may be said to be.

There are, for Kant, two species of sense objects,[184]
according to which the whole of nature as phenomena is
divided.

Now Nature, in this sense of the word, has two
n divisions, in accordance with the main distinction
our sensibility, one of which co prises the objects
the outer, the other the object of the inner; thus
dering possible a two-fold doctrine of Nature, the
DOCTRINE OF BODY and the DOCTRINE OF SOUL, the first
Lin with extended, and the second with thinking,
ure.   185

Here Kant is referring to inner sense in the nar-

ing, a point which he makes clear in his subsequent

at all matter as such is lifeless.

Now we know no other internal principle of
ubstance to change its state but desire, and no
er internal activity whatever but thought, with
t which depends upon it, feeling of pleasure and
a, and impulse or will. But these grounds of
ermination and action in no wise belong to the
sentations of the external sense.   186

It is, then, a propos to enquire whether the objects

sense can be objects for scientific study in the

that external or spatially related objects can be.

cience would be a physiology of inner sense.

If our knowledge of thinking beings in general,
means of pure reason, were based on more than the
ito, if we likewise made use of observations con-
ning the play of our thoughts and the natural laws
the thinking self to be derived from these thoughts,
re would arise an empirical psychology, which would
a kind of physiology of inner sense, capable per-
s of explaining the appearances of inner sense, but
er of revealing such properties as do not in any
belong to possible experience. . . . 187

Kant's hesitancy about affirming such a science is

in this statement, for the sufficient reason that

of the appearances of inner sense.

> If we compare the doctrine of the soul as the
> physiology of inner sense, with the doctrine of the
> body as a physiology of the object of the outer senses,
> we find that while in both much can be learnt empiri-
> cally, there is yet this notable difference. In the
> latter science much that is a priori can be syntheti-
> cally known from the mere concept of an extended
> impenetrable being, but in the former nothing what-
> soever that is a priori can be known synthetically
> from the concept of a thinking being.    188

The implications of this statement are far-reaching.

Concepts employed in physics are not blind because an in-

tuition is given for them, because in fact appearances are

determined a priori in accordance with the categories.  If

on the other hand, we have inner intuitions to which no

body of a priori synthetic knowledge corresponds, this can

only be because such appearances have not been determined

in accordance with the categories.  The difficulty seems to

be due to Kant's doctrine that inner sense is a perpetual

flux, with nothing permanent in it, and this in turn is

because the appearances of inner sense are in time, and

only in time.

> For space alone is determined as permanent,
> while time, and therefore everything that is in inner
> sense is in constant flux.    189

Alongside this we must place Kant's statement that

if everything in the world is in a flux, and nothing is

permanent, substances are inadmissible, [190] a doctrine of

which he takes advantage in proving the emptiness of the

concept of the soul in rational psychology, where he

to decide whether, as souls, we are permanent or not. .
. . .For since the only permanent appearance which we
encounter in the soul is the representation 'I' that
accompanies and connects them all, we are unable to
prove that this 'I', a mere thought, may not be in
the same state of flux as the other thoughts. . .191

Kant unhesitatingly draws the logical conclusions
n this doctrine, in other parts of the <u>Critique</u>. Since
·192
a itself does not change, but only appearances in time,
ly through the permanent does existence in different
ts of the time-series acquire a magnitude which can be
193
itled duration".  In other words, that which is in time,
only in time, cannot be an object of scientific know-
ge; all alteration, if it is to be perceived as altera-
n, presupposes something permanent in intuition, and
194
inner sense no permanent intuition is to be met with".

But it is an even more noteworthy fact, that
in order to understand the possibility of things in
conformity with the categories, and so to demonstrate
the <u>objective reality</u> of the latter, we need, not
merely <u>intuitions</u>, but intuitions that are in all
cases <u>outer intuitions</u>. When, for instance, we take
the pure concepts of <u>relation</u>, we find, firstly, that
in order to obtain something <u>permanent</u> in intuition
corresponding to the concept of <u>substance</u>, we require
an intuition in space (of matter).   195

It would be quite easy at this point to take the
w that we are faced here with another of supposedly
y cases in which Kant contradicts himself, maintaining

the nature of time to distinguish spatially related objects
from the flux of time in inner sense, and on the other hand
that time itself does not change, but only appearances in
it. In other words, time flows, and it does not flow. It
would be quite impossible to convict Kant of contradiction
here, however, for as has been pointed out above, he does
not say that we ever have an intuition of time only, as an
object or as a sensation; time is only the way in which
some appearances are intuited. Although we are acutely
aware of the passage of time, through the constant flux
of our inner sense, we never perceive time itself flowing.
It is one thing to say that time itself flows, and another
to say, as Kant seems to be doing, that anything, (whether
we call it object or appearance, we shall be hitting wide
of the mark) that is in time alone will be in constant
flux. To say that the essence of time is that it flows,
and to say that the essence of time is such that thing_s
in it flow, or change, is to say two different things.
When Kant says that the continuity of time is a flowing
or a flowing away, he is simply referring to the fact
that there are no gaps or breaks in it. Time itself
cannot flow, for it is not a reality in itself. It is
transcendentally ideal, but also an empirically real way
of intuiting anything that can be given to the senses.
Inner sense gives us a heightened awareness of this way

we have of intuiting, because in inner sense we intuit in this way _and only in this way_. We do not at the same time have intuitions of outer sense, which involve another, quite different, way of intuiting. Thus, through inner sense we become aware of time as a way we have of intuiting, different from space, which is another way. In this manner, the immediate apprehension of time is of fundamental importance to the critical philosophy, revealing as it does one of the transcendental elements of sensibility.

The existence of appearances which are solely in time, and time alone, poses serious problems for Kant, however, ones which he does no more than touch upon in a cursory fashion. For example, it is apparent that the kind of change involved in such purely temporal succession as is exemplified in inner sense will be radically different from the kind of change involved in appearances which are both spatially and temporally related. Strictly speaking, such change cannot be cognized. It is not alteration of something which abides, namely, substance. Kant, himself, clearly recognizes this.

> Although both are appearances, the appearance
> to outer sense has something fixed or abiding which
> supplies a substratum as the basis of its transitory
> determinations and therefore a synthetic concept,
> namely, that of space and of an appearance in space;
> whereas time, which is the sole form of our inner in-
> tuition, has nothing abiding, and therefore yields
> knowledge only of the change of determinations, not
> of any object that can be thereby determined. 196

.e can only coi cli de tlat Kant is using the term appearance ver; loosely, in s,ea'in of a] c ranc s of inner sense, sin e .pe r .c _ ar ore cften spol.en cf by him as deteri inate a,q ar ices, t'e re ilt o synt sis and determination in ccor'a.ce with the categories. The self, of course, as a entity, plays no part in inner sense, except as a "universal correlate of apperception and itself a mere thou_ht. . .a thin_ of undefined signification".[197] Perscnal identity is accounted for by the duration of the human body in sp ce, as an object of outer sense capable of being perceived by others.

> T! us the permaneice of the soul, regarded merely as an object of inner sense, re ains undemonstrated, and indeed i de onstrable. Its permanence during life is, of course, evident *per se*, since the thinkin_ being (as man) is itself likewise an object of the outer senses. 198

Thus apparently nothing is capable of being known about the appearances in the perpetual flux of inner sense, neither the e_o or self, nor the appearances, nor the kind of change which characterizes them. Since we are directly aware of them, the status of these things is not quite the same as that of things-in-themselves; nevertheless, they are equally as in eter inate as things-in-t'emselves. The things of which we feel that we are ost intimately aware are not objects of knowledge. It is characteristic of Kant's honesty as a thinker that he does not boggle at this result,

t unwav ringly points out the reasons why, according to
is principles, this must be so, in his analysis of the
claims of psycholo y to be a science. His most important
point is that:

> . . .as in every natural doctrine only so
> much science proper is to be met with therein as
> there is cognition _a priori_, a doctrine of nature
> can only contain so much science proper as there
> is in it of applied mathematics.   199

Kant goes on to point out that mathematics is
"inapplicable to the p enomena of the internal sense and
its laws", for in it all that mathematics could lay hold
200
of would be the law of permanence in the flow of its internal changes. We are able to get as much knowledge
about the soul from this, as we could get, for example, in
geometry merely from the properties of a straight line.
In short, Kant implies, the knowledge we can get is very
little.

This point is scarcely less important than the next
one which Kant raises, namely, that 'the manifold of internal
observation is only separated in thought, but cannot be kept
201
separate and be connected again at pleasure'.  It is to be
noted that both of these shortcomings are due to that very
perpetuity of flux in inner sense, which Kant has so often
himself pointed out, and which lies at the very base of
the whole critical philosophy, in that it allows Kant to
maintain that time is the form of inner sensibility.

## 169

But it cannot be said that Kant has fully appreciated the implications of his own criticism of psychology. If there is no a priori knowledge of the phenomena of inner sense, they can hardly be phenomena at all in the usual Kantian sense. Our means of knowledge of phenomena can always be traced back to the a priori determination of phenomena in accordance with the categories. If we cannot get knowledge in a certain sphere of appearance, it can only be because these appearances have somehow arisen without being subject to determination through the categories under the transcendental unity of apperception. In that case they are not objects of possible experience, in the sense of empirical knowledge. And since the categories provide the ground of all determination of the existence of appearances, the appearances of inner sense cannot even exist as objects of knowledge connected by definite rules to other objects of knowledge. But since these inner appearances most manifestly do exist, a point which Kant never denies, their existence must be radically different from appearances in the more usual sense of appearances subject to determination in accordance with the categories.

Now the existence of these appearances is intimately bound up with time, another point which Kant never fails to stress. If we did not have an awareness of the difference

botweeo th y int it ur i r st t , d t o y we
intuit s tially xten oo ct , there l be o ss-
ibility of disti uirhin between forms of e silility t
all. For if s c d ti e r or o sibility,
we aro ot re f t e difference oetteen one mode of
sensiole intuition nd t ot r, te co lc ot distin uish
between s tial te or l determanati ns t all. There
could, in short, be o transcend nt l aesthetic as ap lied
to human faculties. Thus t c i ediate ap rehension of
time as a for of sensibility is essential to I nt's
philosophy.

     I nt l s offered a solution to the problem of the
fundamental distinction between s ace c time in terms
of forms of sensibility, which involves at t e very least
a recognition of the intimate relation betwee ti e and
the flux of inner experience, and hence of the relevance
of the psyc olo y of inner states to the deter ination
of the nature of ti e. Kent's view thot psycholo y can
never be anything ore tha an a roximately syste atic,
historical descri tion of inner sens , r t cr than
a science, points to the eculiar role that time plays
in Kant's philoso ay. ot only re those a earances
which are in time alone incapable of bein co nized,
but time itself cannot be represe ted in t ou ht. e are
aware of time as a form of sensibility, but we cannot

obtain   conce>tion of it.

> ,ven tir  itseli \ c >os re resent,
> save in so far 's  e  ttenc, in the <u>drawing</u> of
> a strai ht line ( ï ich  as to serv;  s t e outer
> fi urative re resentation of ti.ie), merely to the
> act of the synthesis of the  anifold whereby we
> successively determine inner sense, and in so
> doin; attend to the succession of this determination
> in inner sense.  203

Kant ap arently hold: that thi  figurative repre-

sentation is a le;itimate one, but he passes over in silence

why this, accor( in  to 'is ,rinci,les, must be so, just as

he ignores for the most part the striking difference between

substance as it fi;ures in outer sense, and substance as

a possible concept a plicable to the flux of inner sense.

The essential characteristic of substance in outer sense

is that it is capable neither of increase nor diminution;

hence the a[plication of the concept of quantity to it is

possible only throu;h the a; re;ate of parts outside one

another.  But only in space can we have parts outside one

another, and if we atte. .t to extend the concept of substance

to a sphere which is not in space but only in time, the

concept of quantity cannot apply to substance in this way.

Kant atte.ipts to preserve some meanin; to the concept of

substance in inner sense, by applying his conception of

intensive magnitude.

> That, on the contrary which is considered
> as object of the internal sense .iay have a quantity
> as substance <u>not</u> <u>consisting</u> of <u>rarts</u> <u>outside</u> <u>one</u>
> <u>another</u>, whose parts are therefore not substances,
> whose origination or annihilation therefore need
> not be the ori in tion or annihilation of a substance. 204

## 172

This kind of substance, if indeed, it could be
called a substance at all, has nothing in common with that
of outer sense, a point which Kant makes clear when he
says of the ego, as object of consciousness, that it is a
"thing of undefined signification, namely, the subject of
all predicates without any condition distinguishing this
presentation of the subject from a something generally,
in short, substance, of which no conception of what it is
(is conveyed) through this expression".[205] Altogether,
Kant's attempt to grapple with this problem, namely, of
what meaning the categories can have for the appearances
of inner sense, is highly ambiguous.  On the one hand, Kant
does not want to admit that the soul is a substance, its
liability to destruction seeming to endanger the principle
of the permanence of substance.  Yet, at the same time, he
seems to want to be able to apply the concept of quantity
to inner states, in respect of intensive magnitude.

> Thus consciousness, in other words, the clear-
> ness of the presentations of my soul. . .has a _degree_
> that may be greater or smaller, without to this end
> any substance requiring to arise or be annihilated. [206]

Those sensations of outer sense may legitimately
admit of intensive magnitude, according to Kant, since
they are only states of substance that change, while the
substance remains the same.  Their arising and dying away
cannot affect the permanence of substance.  The appearances

of inner sense, however, are in constant flux; there is no
underlyin  per anence; they are not states of so ething
else that never chan es.  Their arisin  and perishing
throu.l v .ic s de re s is not the  ere _state_ _of_ _chan_ e of
somethin. t at endures; it is a genuine arisin. and perishing, not explicable at all in ter.s of substance, in
short, the very pass .e of time itself, as revealed in
inner sense.

Kant has bou ht the neans of distinguishing between
space and time at a rather expensive price, in terms of
the generality of his theory of knowledge.  Tine is, indeed,
clearly distin.uished from space in that appearances in it
are beyond the pale of co nition, but Kant has accepted a
point of fundamental importance in Bergson's theory of
time, namely, that we are aware of it through inner experience.  For  ant, we are aware of time merely as the
_form_ in which our inner experience is solely conditioned,
but not as an all-encompassing reality.  Yet in respect
of the all-pervasiveness of time, Kant's views are not
entirely dissimilar to those of Bergson, for, as we have
seen, time, for Kant, is the medium by means of which the
categories determine objects and bring about order throughout the phenomenal world.  In addition, the appearances in
time alone bear a strong similarity to things-in-themselves,
(the ultimately real which we know only as appearance),

in that both are indeterminate and unknowable by means of
concepts.  Before taking up these points,  however, we must
examine  Bergson's position on the immediate apprehension
of time.

Bergson also distinguishes between inner sense and
outer sense, although, for him, the distinction is less
sharp than it is for Kant.  The spatially extended is, in
Bergson's view, something quite different, indeed, radically different from what is revealed by the deepest in-
trospection.  But the transition from what is absolutely
outer to what is absolutely inner in intuition is blurred,
for Bergson; the transition involves intermediate states,
unlike Kant's sharp dichotomy.

> When, with the inner regard of my consciousness,
> I examine my person in its passivity, like some super-
> ficial encrustment, first I perceive all the percep-
> tions which come to it from the material world.  These
> perceptions are clear-cut, distinct, juxtaposed or
> mutually juxtaposable; they seek to group themselves
> into objects.  Next I perceive memories more or less
> adherent to these perceptions and which serve to in-
> terpret them; these memories are, so to speak, as if
> detached from the depth of my person and drawn to
> the periphery by perceptions resembling them; they
> are fastened on me without being absolutely myself.
> And finally, I become aware of tendencies, motor habits,
> a crowd of virtual actions more or less solidly bound
> to those perceptions and these memories. . .But if I
> pull myself from the periphery towards the centre, if
> I seek deep down within me what is most uniformly,
> the most constantly and durably myself, I find some-
> thing altogether different.
> What I find beneath these clear-cut crystals
> and this superficial congelation is a continuity of
> flow comparable to no other flowing I have ever seen. 207

## 175

Bergson announces the same fact about inner experience as does Kant.  His exposition differs only in that while Kant was not particularly at pains to communicate the exact character of this internal flux, speaking of it in terms of phenomena and appearances, which strictly speaking, as determinate entities cannot figure in the flux at all, Bergson exerts all his literary powers to try to make us see what sort of thing this inner flow is.  His works are replete with metaphorical devices and figurative language quite consciously used in an attempt to express the quality of this inner flux.  This technique was necessitated by the kind of philosophy Bergson desired to expound, rather than by a mere personal preference for the niceties of literary style.  On the contrary, for Kant, such a manner of exposition was out of the question, not merely because it was foreign to his cast of mind, but for the reason that he wished to lay the ground-work of philosophy in an exact conceptual scheme which would deserve the name of science.  Bergson's view that "metaphysics is. . . the science which claims to dispense with symbols",[208] set him on a path that Kant could not have followed without abandoning his most cherished hopes in philosophy.  It is not surprising, therefore, to find that Kant on the theoretical side of his philosophy says very little about the character of the flux of inner states.  Even though he made

the same point that Bergson does, namely, that inner experience yields an awareness of time, beyond the bare fact
of this, necessary for the exposition of the elements of
transcendental aesthetic, 'ant could say nothing further.
The essential point in this is that ,ant's theory of time
points in a direction in which Kant was unwilling to go.

This refusal to envisage further development is,
of course, bound up with Kant's whole view of human knowledge as unable to extend beyond a possible experience
defined, in effect, by the scope of the applicability of
the categories, limited, in fact, by the kind of categories hant deduced from the forms of judgment he expounded
as the basis of transcendental logic.  Yet hant himself
raises certain problems which could only be answered by
taking this flux of inner states more seriously, and of
these one concerns the relation between inner sense in
the narrow meaning and inner sense in the wide meaning,
or, briefly, the relation between inner sense and outer
sense and the two forms of sensibility, time and space.
How is it possible that these two disparate kinds of sensibility become combined in one unified experience, in
which the intimate relation between them as exhibited in
motion is evident?  One might put this in Kantian terms
and ask, "How is change in general possible?".  It is to be
noted that this question concerns not motion alone, but

. ..ant has dealt with the concept of motion as,
ion, it is needed for natural science, in is
l Foundations of Natural Science, but his de-
presuppose that change is possible, (something,
which no one will doubt, even though it may be
to understand in terms of concepts how it is
Such a question demands an answer showing not
space and time are related to change but also
logically, inner sense is related to outer sense.
rn involves a more exact explanation of how that
ideas" which Stout maintained is absolutely in-
e to the perception of time is related to the per-
space. But the answer to the psychological
ill no doubt turn on the doctrine of what is re-
inner experience, in other words, the nature of
f. At any rate, as to the relation between the
of sensibility, Kant flatly refuses to give an

The much discussed question of the communion
en the thinking and the extended, if we leave
all that is merely fictitious, comes then simply
is; how in a thinking subject outer intuition,
y, that of space, with its filling-in of shape
otion, is possible. And this is a question which
n can possibly answer.   209

nt's refusal is, of course, again dictated by
l theory of knowledge, but that he has seen the
n its generality is indicated by the following

## 178

> Consequently, the question is no longer of the
> communion of the soul with other known substances of
> a different kind outside us, but only of the connection
> of the representations of inner sense with the modi-
> fications of our outer sensibility -- as to how these
> can be so connected with each other according to
> settled laws that they exhibit the unity of a coherent
> experience.   210

Whether Kant's position, in refusing to deal with problems raised by his theory of space and time, is a justifiable one, need not concern us here.  Our present purpose is merely to point out that Kant's theory seems to point in the direction of a further development which could deal with such questions,- one which, however, would have been impossible for Kant, but which could have been carried out by a thinker willing to follow the implications of it beyond the limiting scope of Kant's categorical scheme.

Without undue anticipation, it can be said here that Bergson's theory deals with just those questions which Kant would not attempt to answer, deals with them, moreover, in a way which stems from a basic position similar in many ways to Kant's.  He agrees with Kant, in effect, that the understanding does influence inner sense, producing definite determinations in it of objects and spatial representations. But for him this function of the understanding has a meaning profoundly different from that involved in Kant's philosophy. Bergson gives us a different interpretation of the spatial representation of time, one which allows him to go beyond

## 179

Kant in his theory of the relationship betw en space and
time.  For example, Bergson attempts to explain the relation between inner and outer sense; he attempts to tell
us how it is that we have spatial perceptions and what is
the relation of these to time.  And this involves his
placing a much greater emphasis on the significance of intuition for metaphysics, a development which Kant would
probably have rejected as <u>schwärmerei</u>, but one which,
nevertheless, is a development from Kant's own assumptions
concerning space and time.

For Bergson, inner experience reveals the ongoing
flow of <u>duration</u> itself, a term which Bergson uses to distinguish his intuition of time from the "spatialized" time,
conceived by the understanding.  Time, for Bergson, is not
a conceptualized entity, not a thing-in-itself, conceived
in general terms; it is the reality of concretely felt
change, and this change can best be felt when the intellect does not interfere to separate the continuous flux
into separate states.

> Pure duration is the form which the succession
> of our conscious states assumes when our ego lets
> itself <u>live</u> , when it refrains from separating its
> present state from its former states.   211

In other words, the succession of conscious states
cannot be apprehended in terms of concepts, a point which
Kant also mentions in saying that "the manifold of internal observation is only separated in thought".  212

## 180

Just as, for Kant, there is no underlying permanence in inner sense, so also for Bergson the reality uncovered in inner experience is not a change of the state of some underlying substratum.

> There are changes, but there are underneath the change no things which change; change has no need of a support.     213

With Kant, the "parts" of that which changes in consciousness are not parts outside of one another, such as we find in spatially related objects of outer sense. This is also Bergson's view.

> Thus I said that several conscious states are organized into a whole, permeate one another, gradually gain a richer content, and might thus give anyone ignorant of space the feeling of pure duration; but the very use of the word "several" shows that I had already isolated these states, externalized them in relation to one another, and, in a word, set them side by side; thus, by the very language which I was compelled to use, I betrayed the deeply ingrained habit of setting out time in space.     214

The above quotation also indicates the similarity to Kant, which has been mentioned above, namely, that in order to obtain a representation of time, of the form of our inner experience, we must resort to representing it in spatial terms.  Another similarity is that both Kant and Bergson have recourse to the notion of intensive magnitudes in referring to the succession of psychic states, although Bergson doubts whether this concept is legitimate.

## 181

> · Pure duration, that which consci)usness per-
> ceives, must thus be reckoned among the so-called
> intensive magnitudes, if intensities can be called
> magnitudes: strictly speaking, however, it is·not a
> quantity, and as soon as we try to measure it, we
> unwittingly replace it by space.    215

It is clear that Kant and Bergson have the same thing in mind in incorporating into their philosophies the doctrine of an intimate association between time and inner experience,- they have the same thing in mind in the sense that they have the same phenomenc:, (in the non-Kantian sense) in mind.  It should be added, however, that Bergson develops the implications of this phenomenon further than does Kant.  Thus, for Bergson, duration as revealed in inner experience is an all-encompassing, basic reality. And the reasons for this further development, the sources, that is, from which it springs as an answer to perplexing problems, and the next step in their solution, given the basic premises, is to be found in the relation of the understanding to space, and the doctrine of the cognitive representation of time, topics to be pursued in subsequent sections.

## 182

## 2.  The Cognitive Representation of Time

In one way, Bergson and Hegel represent an interesting contrast of development from Kant, which we may mention
in order to bring out the character of Bergson's development.
They both take a point of departure from Kant's doctrine of
judgment, and both find in this doctrine an inadequacy
amounting to artificiality.  The traditional formal logic,
a cornerstone of Kant's system, and for him, a "closed and
completed body of doctrine",[216]  Hegel calls "the lifeless
bones of a skeleton".[217]  And Bergson, as we shall see, affirms
the inability of the intellect to come to grips with the
primordial flow of time.  Hegel's method of attacking this
problem was to invent a new logic, and a "concrete" doctrine
of judgment.  Bergson's method on the other hand is to accept the inadequacy of the intellect and to push the opposition between the intellect and concrete becoming to its
very limit.  Hegel does not repudiate the importance of
judgment, but develops it.  Bergson not only rejects judgment as a method of knowing reality, but allows the significance of judgment itself to recede, and tries to place
the main emphasis of intellectucal thinking on the spatial
concept.  In developing a position, the seeds of which are
implicit in Kant's theory of time and inner sense, Bergson
finds it necessary to take Kant's doctrine of judgment less

seriously, and to make of it a matter in which static concepts rather th n active judgments are emphasized.  Instead of accepting Kant's doctrine of judgment and its applicability to time, Bergson, in effect, denies it and makes it far more artificial in its relation to the reality of becoming than it was in the philosophy of Kant.  We have now to examine Bergson's reasons for doing this.

We have seen that it is essential to Kant's position that the categories should apply directly to time itself.  This necessarily involves the point that the cognitive representation of time should be legitimate.  In this regard , we find Kant, with typical candour, accepting on the one hand that the flux of inner sense is beyond the .  of cognition, and on the other that time may be given a representation in terms of concepts applicable to outer sense.

'Time is nothing but the form of inner sense, that is, of the intuition of ourselves and of our inner state. . .And just because this inner intuition yields no shape, we endeavour to make up for this want by analogies.  We represent the time-sequence by a line progressing to infinity, in which the manifold constitutes a series of one dimension only; and we reason from the properties of this line to all the properties of time, with this one exception, that while the parts of the line are simultaneous the parts of time are always successive.  From this fact also, that all the relations of time allow of being expressed in an outer intuition, it is evident that the representation is itself an intuition.    218

What is involved in this spatial representation of time?  First of all, there is the conception of both space

and time as homogeneous, made up of units, as it were, which
are all the same.  Kant, indeed, rejects the view that there
are <u>ultimate</u> simples, but nevertheless in speaking of space
and time as <u>quanta</u> <u>continua</u> he reveals the element of homogeneity in his conception of them.

> Space and time are <u>quanta</u> <u>continua</u>, because
> no part of them can be given save as enclosed between
> limits (points or instants), and therefore only in
> such fashion that this part is itself again a space
> or a time.  Space therefore consists solely of spaces,
> time solely of times.   219

The very fact that he conceives of points and instants
as <u>limits</u> implies that every determinate part of space is a
part of the same medium, space, and every determinate length
of time is a part of time.  The homogeneity of these media
is necessary to Kant, otherwise he could never speak of the
"manifold (and) homogeneous in intuition in general". [220] It
is necessary, according to Kant, in order to obtain a conception of space and time to <u>construct</u> these concepts,
and this, of course, involves intuition.

> The only intuition that is given <u>a</u> <u>priori</u> is
> that of the mere form of appearances, space and time.
> A concept of space and time, as quanta, can be exhi-
> bited <u>a</u> <u>priori</u> in intuition, that is, constructed,
> either in respect of quality (figure) of the quanta,
> or through number in their quantity only (the mere
> synthesis of the homogeneous manifold).   221

But the manner in which Kant describes how the
elementary conceptions of space and time are formed reveals
that in the formation of these concepts the successiveness

time, itself, is cancelled, and left out.  Synthesis of

homogeneous manifold, even though it is always succes-

e, for Kant, involves holding together in thought all

parts which are successively synthesized.

When I seek to draw a line in thought, or to
think of the time from one noon to another, or even
to represent to myself some particular number, obviously the various manifold representations that are
involved must be apprehended by me in thought one
after another.  But if I were always to drop out of
thought the preceding representations, (the first
parts of the line, the antecedent parts of the time
period, or the units in the order represented), and
did not reproduce them while advancing to those that
follow, a complete representation would never be obtained: none of the above-mentioned thoughts, not
even the purest and most elementary representations
of space and time could arise.  222

Bergson's analysis of the concept of number is

ikingly similar to that of Kant.  For both, number in-

ves synthesis.  "Number", Bergson tells us, "may be de-

ed in general as a collection of units, or, speaking

e exactly, as the synthesis of the one and the many".

gson also draws attention to the point Kant has made,

aly, that all the parts of the successive synthesis

t be held together, as it were, simultaneously in

ught.

For if we picture to ourselves each of the sheep
in the flock in succession and separately, we shall
never have to do with more than a single sheep.  In order that the number should go on increasing in pro-
portion as we advance, we must retain the successive
images and set them alongside of each of the new units

which we picture to ourselves: now it is in space that such a juxtaposition takes place and not in pure duration.  In fact, it will be easily granted that counting material objects means thinking all these objects together, thereby leaving them in space. 224

It may be thought that here Bergson has passed rather hastily from the point that the units cannot be dropped out of thought to the point that they must therefore be left in space.  But the passage from the one to the other is not performed without argument, and in this respect again Bergson follows Kant.  For Bergson agrees with Kant that mathematical concepts require an intuition. Abstract numbers, as symbols, are not even thought, but are merely expressions of number useful for reckoning.

> It will be seen that we began by imagining e.g. a row of balls, that these balls afterwards became points, and, finally, this image itself disappeared, leaving behind it, as we say, nothing but abstract number.  But at this very moment we ceased to have an image or even an idea of it; we kept only the symbol which is necessary for reckoning and which is the conventional way of expressing number.  For we can confidently assert that 12 is half of 24 without thinking either the number 12 or the number 24: indeed, as far as quick calculation is concerned, we have everything to gain by not doing so.  225

Kant constantly emphasizes the point that geometry requires an intuition of space, and indeed cannot proceed at all without this intuition.  It is Kant's view that all of mathematics requires an intuitive element; one cannot arrive at the synthetic _a priori_ propositions of mathematics by the mere analysis of concepts.

## 187

Mathematics, as synthetic cognition _a
priori_ , is only possible by referring to no other
objects than those of the senses. At the basis of
their empirical intuition lies a pure intuition (of
space and time) which is _a priori_. 226

e have already seen that the schema of quantity
is number and that number, for Kant, always involves a
successive synthesis.  Even geometry, in dealing with line
planes, figures, etc. requires a successive synthesis.

I cannot represent to myself a line, however
small, without drawing it in thought, that is, generating from a point all its parts one after another.
Only in this way can the intuition be obtained.  227

The mathematics of space (geometry) is based
upon this successive synthesis of the productive imagination in the generation of figures.  228

Unfortunately, Kant here omits mentioning the
point that the synthesis must be _held together_ in thought,
and that the units of the homogeneous cannot be dropped
out as they would be if the intuition were _solely_ successive.  We cannot help wondering what the character of this
product of synthesis is, and whether it would be correct
to call it spatial rather than temporal.  There is some
evidence that Kant, himself, did not think of it as temporal.  He tells us that we cannot conceive alteration
without having recourse to intuition,- "The intuition
required is the intuition of the movement of a point in
space".  229
Kant seems to be saying that it is just the peculiar property of space that things in it can _coexist_,

which implies that in our conception of space things are
held together in the f shion he has said is necessary even
for "the most elementary representations" of space _and
time_. "space alone is determined as permanent, while
time, and therefore everything that is in inner sense is
in constant flux".[230] Kant held that alteration is only conceivable as alteration of substance, a permanent element
which persists through changes of state. It s ems clear
that Kant thou ht of this permanent element as space itself,
or rather the permanence of the real in space, which, of
course, i plies the permanence of space. We have already
noted that the substance of outer sense is quite unlike
anything that could be said to be a substance in inner
sense. Kant reaffirms this difference in a passage which
reveals not only that _because_ of the perpetuity of the
flux of inner sense, we cannot obtain an immediate representation of time, but also that we can obtain a mediate,
spatial representation of time _because_ of the permanence
or "held-togetherness" of space.

> For in order that we may afterwards make inner
> alterations likewise thinkable, we must represent time
> (the form of inner sense) figuratively as a line, and
> the inner alteration through the drawing of this line
> (motion), and so in this manner by means of outer in-
> tuition make comprehensible the successive existence
> of ourselves in different states. The reason of this
> is that ll alteration, if it to be perceived as al-
> teration, presupposes something permanent in intuition,
> and that in inner sense no permanent intuition is to
> be met with.    [231]

Th  exte t to w ich intellectu l o erations presuppose sp ce, for  ant, if at  ll, is a point  ' ich we
shall consi er later.  ..e wish here merely to draw attention to th  point t'at  ant's fi urative, spatial repre-
senation of ti e l aves out  hat he  i self considers to
be th  essential difference  etween space and time, na ely,
the succ ssiv ness of ti e.  For althou h  ant hol's that
we can repres t  tine by a l  ie, and reason from the properties of t is line to the properties of time, he also
says that the alteration of in er  ense, nd hence the
intrinsic c iaracter of ti e itself, can only be intuited
in _motion._  .er  a ain, it is apparent that  ant is using
a term applic le to outer sense, _n  _ely, alteration,
rather loosely with res ect to in er sense.  The flux of
inner sense c n  properly be called alteration, for as
 ant has ve e ently asser ed, t ere is not in  permanent
in inner sense _to alter._

It  ay see  d fficult to rec cile  ant's affir-
mation of the permanence of spatial determinations, or of
perma ence in and through spatial deter inations, with his
view that all outer appearances are the result of a successive synthesis of the productive i agination.  It should
be noted, however, that there is nothing necessari y inconsistent in holdin  these t o positions together. The

successive synthesis of the roductive  imaination, as a
transcendental condition of appearances, cannot, indeed,
be considered to be an _event_, which has occurred, or does
repeatedly occur, a view which is associated with the opinion
that Kant is doing genetic psychology, a gross misinter-
pretation of him. Nor can it be considered to be noumenal
or outside of time. Here we agree with Paton, who says:

> . . .I do find it difficult to suppose. . .that
> our minds are such that to them reality must appear,
> not only as a succession of changes in time, but as a
> succession of changes in time which must conform to
> causal law.
> There are two ways of avoiding this difficulty.
> One is to assert that the transcendental synthesis of
> which Kant speaks is a pre-conscious and noumenal syn-
> thesis which somehow constructs the whole physical
> world for us before we begin to know it. For this
> view I can find no basis in Kant, nor does it seem to
> me to have the least plausibility as a metaphysical
> theory. 232

The transcendental synthesis must therefore be a
continuous process _in_ time. Only this, incidentally, will
suffice as a basis of a refutation of Hume. Now it is not
inconsistent to suppose that in so far as time itself, as
a whole, is a permanent reality, i.e. an eternal process,
it should continue to synthesize quanta of space, which
would correspond to the permanence of time itself. Accordingly, the schema of substance, the permanence of the real
in time, would be a condition not derived from space, but
_imposed_ on space, through the very continuity of the successiveness of the synthesis. Thus the logical ground of the

princi le o.  '    .  . t.ce o. .ub.t nce .o.ld be expresse
in experi.nce .. t.  , rma. ence o^ ti.e i.self.  .nd t'is
is quite in accord . it  .hat .ant  ys  bo. t it.

.er.a.ence, as the abiding correlate of all
existence of appearances, of all change and all con-
co.itance, ex.resses ti.e i. general.  .or change
does not affect ti.e itself, but only appearances
in tine.    233

In a.ditio., t.ere are two reasons .l.y this per-
menence of ti.e .ust oe expressed i. outer sense rat.er
than in i...r se.se.  .he first is that ti.e itself cannot be perceived.  .ence the permanence of ti.e itself
cannot be im.edia.tely presented.  .ie second reason, and
perha.s the .ore fundam..ntal o.e, is t.at .he succession
or constan. flux of appearances ..n time alone preclu.es
their .ivin. a representation of the permanence of ti.e
itself.  Obviously, the permanence of ti.e itself can.ot
be expressed or un.krstood by means of ap.earances (representations) .hic. are in .ine alone, for the essential
of ti.e is i.s successive.ess.  It is the for.al condition
of all series.  T'us .he per.anence of .ine as a condition
of the possibility of ex.erience ca. only be .no.m by .ean
of re..usenta.ions pertainin. to a.other, different r.ediun
which is in i.self .ot i..tri.sically successive.

.ut .s the parts of space are co-ordinated
with, .ot subordinated to, one a.other, one part is
not t..e co.dition of the possibility o. another; and
unli.e ti.e, space does not i. itself consitute a

series.  Nevertheless the synthesis of the manifold
parts of space, by means of which we apprehend space,
is successive, taking place in time and containing a
series.    234

e can conclude, then, that the cognitive repre-

sentation of space is a representation of space as a medium

in which the parts are co-existent.  "For as its parts are

co-exi tent, it is on a gregate, not a series".[235]  e can

see also, that even though any magnitude whatsoever is the

result of a synthesis, the _representation_ of that magnitude

must be as permanent, or at least as co-existing, held-

together, in the representation.

> Only through the permanent does existence in
> different parts of the time-series acquire a magnitude
> which can be entitled duration.  For in bare succession
> existence is always vanishing and recommencing, and
> never has the least magnitude.    236

From all this it is apparent that spatial concep-

tions do not and cannot represent the intrinsic nature of

time as we are aware of it in inner sense.  Kant has ad-

mitted this much in the immediately foregoing quotation.

But it is just this difference between space and time of

which Bergson takes advantage in his arguments against the

spatializing of time.  There are two kinds of multiplicity,

Bergson tells us, one kind applicable to space, and another

kind, radically different, applicable only to time.

## 193

Our final conclusion, therefore, is that there
are two kinds of multiplicity: that of material objects,
to which the conception of number is immediately applicable; and the multiplicity of states of consciousness,
which cannot be regarded as numerical without the help
of some symbolical representation, in which a necessary element is space.   237

In admitting that in bare succession, there is never the least magnitude, Kant has, in effect, admitted that
the concept of number applicable to outer sense in inapplicable to the states of inner sense.  For he makes clear
that a neces ary presupposition of counting is unity,  and [238]
it is hard to see how there can be numerical unity where
there is not the least magnitude.  Both Kant and Bergson,
indeed, affirm that the ultimate ground of unity lies in
a pure act of the mind, and that the material on which this
pure act is brought to bear is a homogeneous manifold.

What must first be given--with a view to the
a priori knowledge of all objects-- is the manifold
of pure intuition; the second factor involved is the
synthesis of this manifold by means of the imagination.  But even this does not yield knowledge.  The
concepts which give unity to this pure synthesis,
and which consist solely in the representation of
this necessary synthetic unity, furnish the third
requisite for the knowledge of an object;  and they
rest on the understanding.   239

For Bergson, the only kind of unity is unity introduced by a simple act of the mind:

Nevertheless, by looking more closely into the
matter, we shall see that all unity is the unity of a
simple act of the mind, and that, as this is an act of
unification, there must be some multiplicity to
unify.   240

## 194

The unity wlich the mind introduces i. plies, for
Ber son, if not synthesis, at least the continuity of multiplicity.

> You will never get out of an idea which you
> have formed anytling which you have not put into it;
> and if the unity by means of which you make up your
> number is the unity of an act and not of an object,
> no effort of analysis will bring out anything but
> unity pure and simple. No doubt, when you equate the
> number 3 to the sum of 1 + 1 + 1 nothing prevents
> you from regarding the units which compose it as in-
> divisible: but the reason is that you do not choose
> to make use of the multiplicity which is enclosed
> within each of these units. 241

Bergson agrees with Kant that numbers are reached
by a successive process of thought which reaches the final
result by going through a series of units. The units seem
to be indivisible while the process of synthesis is going
on, and indeed, because we choose to regard them as separate units for the purpose of synthesizing them. But the
final result is a unity in which all discontinuity of the
synthesized units is merged in the unity of the synthesized
number.

> Again; if we form the same number with halves,
> with quarters, with any units whatever, these units,
> in so far as they serve to form the said number, will
> constitute elements which are provisionally indivisible;
> and it is always by jerks, by sudden jumps, so to speak,
> that we advance from one to the other. And the reason
> is that, in order to get a number, we are compelled to
> fix our attention successively on each of the units of
> which it is compounded. . .And when we look at humber
> in its finished state, this union is an accomplished
> fact: the points have become lines, the divisions have
> been blotted out, the whole displays all the charac-
> teristics of continuity. 242

## 195

In speaking of the synthesis implied in the addition of seven and five, Kant draws attention to the single unified synthesis of each number itself.

> But although the proposition (7 + 5 = 12) is synthetic it is also only singular. So far as we are here attending merely to the synthesis of the homogeneous (of units), that synthesis can take place only in one way, although the _employment_ of these numbers is general.    243

But the singular unity of number is quite inapplicable to the perpetual flux of inner sense, for the units, (if they can be called units) which flow through inner sense cannot be held together in a final synthesis.  They are, as Kant says, _dropped_ _out_ _of_ _thought_ by virtue of the fact that they are in time alone.  This, then, is the impasse in which Kant's theory of space and time remains, namely, that while a recognition of the fact of becoming as exemplified in inner experience is necessary in order that Kant should be able to speak of time as the form of inner sense, it is quite impossible to see, in terms of Kant's own explanation of how the concepts of space, ti. , .id number, are formed, how the time of which we are aware as a form of sensibility, can be represented in concepts at all. This may be put in the form of a Bergsonian criticism in the question: if time _is_ adequately represented in spatial terms, how are space and time to be distinguished at all? As we mentioned above, in Chapter Two, Section One, it is

difficult to see how two unique things can h ve anything in common, and t'ereby be mutually understood. But if space and ti_e are to be distinguished as two _different_ forms of intuition, they must at least in so far as their intrinsic properties are concerned, be quite unique. And in this case, for the reasons we have outlined, it will not be pos- sible to say that they can both be adequately represented in concepts whic'1 have anything in common. This, however, is how, according to Kant, it must be; for in referring to how we can have the phenomenal self as an object of con- sciousness, he illustrates this possibility by appealing to the fact that time can only be represented in spatial terms.

> Indeed, that this is how it must be, is easily shown--if we ad.it that space is merely a pure form  of the appearances of outer sense-- by the fact that we' cannot obtain for ourselves a representation of time, which is not an object of outer intuition, except under the image of a line, which we draw, and that by this mode of depcting it alone could we know of the single- ness of its dimension; and similarly by the fact that for all inner perceptions we derive the determination of lengths of time or of points of time from the changes which are exhibited to us in outer things, and that the determinations of inner sense have therefore to be arran.ed as appearances in time in precisely the same manner in which we arrange those of outer sense in space.    244

The illustration, however, does not improve Kant's argument, because both the phenomenal self and the repre- senation of time have exactly the same relation to cognitive

representation.  They  re indeed so closely associated
that to deal with them separately in this case is impossible.  But we have already seen the seriousness of Kant's
own criticism of psychology.  Even if it is granted that
the phenomenal self can be an object of consciousness, it
must be admitted that as an object it is something absolutely different from the objects of outer sense, and cannot be
known by concepts applicable to them.  We have also seen
how necessary it is to Kant's idealism to distinguish the
phenomenal self very sharply from the rest of the phenomenal
world.  Kant, himself, realizes that he cannot by any means
admit the possibility of a materialistic psychology without
endangering his cardinal principle, the transcendental unity
of apperception, and the associated forms of judgment.

In distinguishing between inner sense and pure apperception, Kant has, in effect, opened up the possibility
of the two different lines of development followed by Bergson and Hegel respectively. Since he also made time the
sole form of inner sensibility, Bergson's theory represents
the result of emphasis on our awareness of the flux of inner sense and the removal of this from the sphere of cognition.  For Bergson's main charge against Kant is that he
assumed uncritically that time may be represented in spatial
terms, and that the flux of inner sense may be legitimately spatialized.

## 198

Kant's great mistake was to take time as a homogeneous medium. He did not notice that real duration is made up of moments inside one another, and that when it seems to assume the form of a homogeneous whole, it is because it gets expressed in space. Thus the very distinction which he makes between space and time amounts at bottom to confusing time with space, and the symbolical representation of the ego with the ego itself. He thought that consciousness was incapable of perceiving psychic states otherwise than by juxta-position, forgetting that a medium in which these states are set side by side and distinguished from one another is of course space, and not duration. He was thereby led to believe that the same states can recur in the depths of consciousness, just as the same physical phenomena are repeated in space; this at least is what he implicitly admitted when he ascribed to the causal relation the same meaning and the same function in the inner as in the outer world. 245

What are Bergson's reasons for disagreeing with

Kant? They are, in fact, echoes of the very points we

have made in connection with Kant's recognition of the flux

of inner sense. Bergson points out that ". . .if time, as

immediate consciousness perceives it, were, like space, a

homogeneous medium, science would be able to deal with it,
246
as it can with space".  This point is implied in Kant's

own criticism of psychology. Because everything in inner

sense is in constant flux, the categories cannot deal with

the appearances of inner sense. But not only is empirical

science unable to deal with appearances in time alone,

there is no body of synthetic <u>a priori</u> knowledge, no <u>pure</u>

science, which pertains only to the intuition of time. For

in spite of considerable shifting of ground, Kant was

unable to  oint to any  ody of synthetic _a rriori_ knowledge
which re uires   pure intuition of time, i. the same un-
equivocal an'  lausible way in w i h it is arguable that
geometry presup oses a pure intuition of space.  In the
_Critique_, he aifirms that kinematics, the general doctrine
of motion, is such a science, but it is apparent that motion
requires not a pure intuition but an empirical intuition,
and the introduction of  n enpirical element into t.e science
destroys the very _a priori_ element which the science is to
contain.  In the _Prolegomena_, Kant suggests that both the
doctrine of motion and arithmetic require pure intuitions
of time.  Paton, who says that "the temporal science parallel
to geometry is, at best, a trifle shadowy",[247] elucidates
the difficulties which Kant has in trying to find such a
science.

> . . . he has to bring in change and motion,
> but change and motion are not wholly free from em-
> pirical elements, and are not on the same footing
> as time and space.  Furthermore the science of
> geometry takes account of space only, whereas the
> doctrine of motion must take account of both space
> and time.  Since time is the form of inner sense,
> a pure science of time should enable us to deal
> _a priori_ with inner states (not with moving bodies),
> and should offer a basis for psychology rather than
> for physics. [248]

Paton adds in a foot-note that "The precise nature
of the 'doctrine of motion' is a further difficulty".[249]
It seems clear that there is no such pure temporal science,
and those properties of time which Kant is able to state
rest on the very spatial analogy which, in terms of his

own osition, is hi,hly uestionable.  But it is not merely
the f<ct th t kant failed to find   ure te oral science
that i  im ort nt here, although t is in itself is signifi-
cant.   h t is perha s ore pertinent is that k nt has
ii self shown the impo sibility of such a science in his
remarks about i ner sense a d its constant flux.

The crux of the problem created by kant's recognition of the flux of inn r sense, and his criticism of
psycholo y as a science, rests in the relation between
inner and outer sense.  It is kant's view that time alone
is  bsolutely all-pervasive in the domain of sense.   ow
how it is  ossible that this for of sensibility should
on the one hand be combined with the other form of sensibility, space, in one area of appearances, and on the other
hand should reserve to itself another area of appearances
which are non-spatial, i difficult to understand.  kant is
emphatic on the point that " here i only one ti e in which
all different ti es must be located, ot as coexistent but
as in succession to one another",²⁵⁰ but he also seems to
recognize "subjective" time.

> In my own consciousness, therefore, identity
> of person is unfailin ly ret with.  But if I view
> myself fro  tl e standpoint of a other person (as an
> object of his outer intuition), it is this outer
> observer who first represents e in time, for in the
> apperception ti e is re resented, strictly speaking,
> only in me.  Although he admits, therefore, the 'I',
> which acc panies, nd indee with co lete identity,
> all representations at all times in my consciousness,
> he will draw no inference from this to the objective
> permanence of myself.  For just as the time in which

the observer sets a limit to the time of every involution
of his sensibility,      the immensity which necessarily bound up with my consciousness is not therefore bound up with it' 'is, that is, with the con-
ciousness which contains the outer intuition of my
subject. 251

Kant has here sailed into very treacherous waters.
Questions rise, for example, as to our knowledge of the
existence of other people's minds, and as to whether one
person's subjectivity may be an object for another person,
and so on.  Kant does not enlighten us about such matters,
or even about the possibility of such knowledge.  This
passage, however, does reveal the difficulties which arise
in connection with the relation between inner and outer
sense.  Briefly, we may ask: are we to suppose that the
time of inner sense, (in the narrow meaning) is different
from the time of outer sense?  If not, by what right do
we suppose that the time which is revealed to us as the
distinctive form of the flux of inner sense is identical
with the time of the phenomenal world as it is dealt with
in physics?  This, specifically, was a problem which was
of paramount interest to Bergson.

He notes, first of all, that the time of outer
sense is markedly different from the duration of inner sense.

Now, let us notice that when we speak of time,
we generally think of a homogeneous medium in which
our conscious states are ranged alongside one another
as in space, so as to form a discrete multiplicity.
Would not time, thus understood, be to the multiplicity
of our psychic states what intensity is to certain of
them,- a sign, a symbol, absolutely distinct from true
duration? 252

ne se confonde d'abord pour nous avec la continuité de
notre vie intérieure", and he is speaking here of the
conception of time, that time which we employ to characteriz
external things.   We have already seen why, according
to Kant's principles, the form of inner sense, (in the
narrow meaning) is not representable in terms of number,
and magnitude, i.e. extensiveness, which are concepts applicable to coexistent space.  What, then, are we to conclude?  How does Kant manage legitimately to pass from the
time of inner sense to the time of outer sense, or, in othe
words, to extend the narrow meaning of inner sense to the
wider meaning which includes the whole phenomenal world?
In Bergson's words: "Comment passons-nous de ce temps
intérieur au temps des choses?"   This is the problem implicit in Kant's theory of time which Bergson has set himself to solve.

     Bergson's solution consists in boldly affirming the
metaphysical primacy of the time of inner sense (duration)
and in casting out measured or homogeneous time, as a spurious, (though admittedly useful) conception due to the

conception. He thereby develops Kant's view that time is,
indeed, primary in the domain of sense, but rejects Kant's
view that time is a homogeneous medium. Bergson sees clearly that the recognition of the flux of inner sense makes
it quite impossible to conceive of time as a series, in
which events are placed as points on a line. He admits
that time is successive, but he argues that the successiveness is not adequately represented by spatial analogies.

> . . .real duration is what we have always
> called time, but time perceived as indivisible. That
> time implies succession I do not deny. But that
> succession is first presented to our consciousness,
> like the distinction of a "before" and "after" set
> side by side, is what I cannot admit. When we listen
> to a melody we have the purest impression of succession
> we could possibly have,- an impression as far removed
> as possible from that of simultaneity,- and yet it is
> the very continuity of the melody and the impossibility
> of breaking it up which makes that impression upon
> us.    255

Duration is not successive in a spatial sense, because such a conception of successiveness implies discrete
differences of state, which have some magnitude, and Kant
himself has recognized that there is not the least magnitude in bare succession.

Thus Kant's acceptance of the theory we have called
possibility B lies along the path toward a view of time as
pure becoming, in that since the categories must apply to
time itself, time must be a different medium from space.
But its sole difference from space consists in its

succ ssiv ness, whic , as we have seen, is thot it to consist in t e fact tha, t e ti -series h s n ope end on
whic new eve ts are constantly bei added.  It is clear,
however, that it is the process of beco in, at t e open
end of the series to w ich t e c te ories ust apply if
t ey re to e eter inative of ppearanc s, because, (a)
only in this ay can it be shown that the future in some
respects must resemble the past, and (b) since the extensive continuum of tine is oth rwise indistin uishable from
that of space, a reco nition of becoming would otherwise be
quite impossible.  Both possibil ties A and B reco nize
beco in in tle sane vay, namely, by a conception of a
projecting time-series.  But A conceives this becoming as
a result of the movements of bodies, whereas B accepts
the fact of beconing and attempts to show that certain
principles overn the beco in itself.  ut if it were held
that these principles a plie to the conti uum of that which
has become, either one ust a it that there is no reason
to believe that t e future will resemble the past, or one
must conceive the whole time-series to be completely laid
out and t us deter ined.  T is latter position involves
the complete rejection of t e significance of the temporal
distinctions ade by the self, as well as the experience
of the becoming of things.  nd this is tantu ount to the
theory of the manifold, the difficulties of which we nave

already e in d. In u, c s., 1 is cl    h u  t
Kant did 1 co .1   tl  e perience of beco i  in 'is
remarks about tle flux of in r xperience.

Nevertheless, it is difficult to se 'ow concepts
which are a plicable to th t v ic .as beco.e can e
plicable to ti e as pure beco ing. In 'oldin  that the
categories are sche atised oy eans of time-deter inations,
Kant i lies th t the forus of jud ent are e bodie  in
ti e itself. I tever beco es ust beco e according to
certain eneral deter inative principles.  Thus he calls
the cate ories "rules of synthesis", whic , as it were,
guide the beco ing of thin s alon  certain eneral lines.
This osition bears a certain rese blance to the subjective
aim of hite ead's actual entities.  But whereas Whitehead
tells us t at the actual entity freely chooses its subjective
aim from God, ant does ot tell us ow the categories can
have an indepe dent ori in in the nature of the in , and
can as vell be e bodie  in ti e-deter inations.  hite ead's
view may cr ay not be satisf ctory, but it at least
attempt t reveal ov the beco ing of things is subject
to certain rinci les. The difficulty lies in the iwe oid-
ent ori in of t cate orie.  e ight erha s hold that
thinkin itself is a rocess, (in hich case, as a process
for the whole of re lity, it ould be on-te oral, urely
lo ical, as it is vith e el), and thus retain the essential

point that proc   is gui ed or letu  ined by logical
cate ories.       u it ooe s diffic lt to un rstand how a
temporal process must necessarily be subject to cate-
orical deter  ation if it is also held that these categories have an ori in ind pendent of the process.  e may
well grant the necessity of dealing with the origin of
the categories and ti e, separately for pur ses of exo-
sition, but we cannot hold tht tle two are ulti ately
distinct without r  ing it hard to see how they ever get
together.  kant's Copernican revolution not only requires
that the   st  et together, that is, that the categories
must be deter ir ative of appearances through the medium
of time, but also requires that the categories must arise
independently of the realm of becoming entirely.  Otherwise, he could never hold that they were prior to experience,
which is the locus of becoming.

It see is clear that kant's doctrine of the transcendental ina ination represents an attempt to meet this
very problem.  It is the ima ination which performs the
successive synthesis, and it does so, according to kant,
in conformity with the cate ories.  ut why it _rust_ do so
remains obscure.  Kant simply tells us that:

> The two extremes, namely sensibility and un-
> derstanding, must stand i  necessary connection with
> each other through the mediation of this transcendental
> function of imagination, because otherwise the former,

though i ee yieldi , a pear nces, would supply no
object o irical o led e, conseque tly no
experience. 257

It is clear t at ant can only maintain this view
that empirical no led e _is_ experience if he separates
sensi ility, d nce time, fro the deter i ative principles. In order t slow tle possi ility of synthetic
a _priori_ k owle e, Kant s to found the categories on
an absolutely cert in and unquestionably solid basis. He
did in fact found them on what he took to be a solid basis,
namely, t e forms of jud ient of traditional logic, utilized
with appropriate ch nges. In deriving the principles deter inative of appeararces from a source quite apart from
the world of beco ing, however, Kant created for himself
the problem of how to et the two back together again.
Hence, as well, the doctrine of the schematism, for as
Kant says, "T e sce a is in itself always a product of
258
imagination". ut either the production of schemata by
the transcendental ima ination must have the same apodeictic
certainty as the forms of judgment, in which case the independent origin of the categories is superfl ous, or
there must be so e further determining relation between
the production of schemata and the logical functions of
the understanding. The obscurity of t is relation represents the seed of Bergson's radical separation of the
intellect and time.

## 208

Bergson, in effect, asserts the insolubility of
this problem by declaring that the intellect falsifies
time in attempting to form a concept of it.  Pure duration
eludes conceptualization.  It eludes that very synthesis
which Kant tells us involves holding all the parts synthesized together, and not dropping them out, as they would
be in bare succession.

> There is real duration, the heterogeneous
> moments of which permeate one another; each moment,
> however, can be brought into relation with a state
> of the external world which is contemporaneous with
> it, and can be separated from the other moments in
> consequence of this very process.  The comparison of
> these two realities gives rise to a symbolical re-
> presentation of duration, derived from space.  Dura-
> tion thus assumes the illusory form of a homogeneous
> medium. . . 259

Bergson argues, accordingly, that if there is such
a thing as a synthesis of time, it is not a synthesis which
can be conceived in terms of homogeneous units, but is a
synthesis which is qualitative rather than quantitative.

> Space contains only parts of space, and at
> whatever point of space we consider the moving body,
> we shall get only a position.  If consciousness is
> aware of anything more than positions, the reason is
> that it keeps the successive positions in mind and
> synthesizes them.  But how does it carry out a synthesis
> of this kind?  It cannot be by a fresh setting out of
> these same positions in a homogeneous medium, for a
> fresh synthesis would be necessary to connect the posi-
> tions with one another, and so on indefinitely.  We are
> thus compelled to admit that we have here to do with
> a synthesis which is, so to speak, qualitative, a gra-
> dual organization of our successive sensations, a
> unity resembling that of a phrase in a melody.  260

## 209

It is, for Bergson, forever impossible to understand the reality of temporal process by means of concepts. Metaphysics ust reject the sort of analysis which Kant gives us, and resort to intuition. Of the real duration, Bergson says:

> But still less coul it be represented by <u>concepts</u>, that is, by abstract ideas, whether general or simple. Doubtless no image will quite answer to the original feeling I have of the flowing of myself. But neither is it necessary for me to try to express it. To him who is not c ble of iving himself the intuition of the dur tion constitutive of his being, nothing will ever give it, neither concept nor images.261

It is ap arent that Bergson, too, has accepted the position we have called ossibility (B), but instead of grappling with the problem of how rational principles can be determinative of ocess, he rejects the problem entirely. If we are to under tand how the external world arises from the basic temporal process, we must o so by means of this metaphysical intuition. If it is true of Kant, as Kerp-Smith suggests, that an absolutely fundamental principle of the <u>Critique</u> is that all analysis presupposes a previously exercised synthesis, it is equally true of Bergson that all analysis falsifies the peculiar temporal synthesis, which we apprehend in duration.

> It follows that an absolute can only be given in an <u>intuition</u>, while all the rest has to do with <u>analysis</u>. e call intuition ere the <u>sympathy</u> by which one is transported into the interior of an object in order to coincide with

> what there is unique and consequently inexpressible
> in it.  Analysis, on the contrary, is the operation
> which reduces the object to elements already known,
> that is, common to that object and others.  Analysing
> then consists in expressing a thing in terms of what
> is not it.    263

At the root of Bergson's rejection of a logic of
temporal process is his conception of logical form as an
essentially static thing.  Concepts, for Bergson, and the
logical relations between them, represent the antithesis
of temporal process.  And for Kant, as well, the operations
of the understanding, were, as we have seen, completely
severed from all connection with time, after the period of
the _Inaugural Dissertation_.  It is just for this reason
that it is all the more difficult to see the necessity of
the immanent logic of the production of transcendental
schemata by the transcendental imagination.  Bergson can
congratulate James for having cried out against the "block
universe", can share with James the view that future events
are not determined, just because he denies a logical determination of the passage of time.  And because the reality
of time is known, as it is for Kant, (as a form of sensibility), through inner experience, Bergson can stress this
inner intuition as more important for metaphysics than
conceptual thinking.  At bottom, Bergson's theory of time
represents the results of carrying out the implications of
Kant's distinction between inner sense and apperception.

In distinguishing between the two, Kant did not lay much emphasis on the fact that inner sense is <u>conscious</u> inner sense, in which we are directly aware of the reality of change. It is this fact which Bergson seizes upon and develops. He follows Kant in separating this consciousness from the mere logical identity of the subject, of the thinking subject, and is thus led to the view that this consciousness of change is primary and quite inexplicable in terms of concepts. Let the numerical identity of the self be a logical fiction, a mere symbol imposed on the flow of inner experience. The consciousness of change remains. It follows that the self must be something quite unlike a thinking being, or a logical subject. We thus find Bergson, in effect, <u>defining</u> consciousness in terms of memory and anticipation, which in turn are associated with the temporal distinctions known to the self.

> To create the future requires preparatory action in the present, to prepare what will be is to utilize what has been; life therefore is employed from its start in conserving the past and anticipating the future in a duration in which past, present and future tread one on another, forming an indivisible continuity. Such memory, such anticipation, are consciousness itself. 264

The idealistic element in Kant's thought necessitates a distinction between the self and the material world, which must be reflected in the character of the phenomenal self. His distinction between space and time

as forms of outer and inner sense, respectively, involves
the association of time with inner experience, and also
accomplishes the required separation of the phenomenal
self from the material world. But he has further to separate the logical functions of the understanding from time
and inner sense. His Copernican revolution, however, requires that the categories should apply directly to time.
This creates the problem of how this is possible in view
of the disparity between inner sense and its form, time,
and the logical functions. Kant is also faced with the
problem of how inner sense relates to outer sense. Thus
Kant's distinction between space and time serves several
purposes: (<u>a</u>) it allows him to separate the self from the
material world; (<u>b</u>) it allows a recognition of the immediate
apprehension of becoming; (<u>c</u>) it allows him to hold that
only time is all-pervasive in the domain of sense, which in
turn leads to (<u>d</u>) the doctrine of the application of the
categories to time alone, and hence a complete answer to
Hume. But this necessary mixing of the temporal distinctions made by the self with the view of space and time as
extensive, which is characteristic of the two theories we
have called possibilities A and B, creates for Kant, whose
views follow possibility B, two major problems, which
augur a development in the direction of Bergson's views.
The two points, (<u>a</u>) and (<u>b</u>) provide the seed of Bergson's

durée, a dev lop ent ster in  from the dijinction between
inner sense in the narro  and wide eanings,  nd the problem
posed by t! e fact that inner sense in the narrow meaning
lies outside the pale of co nition.  The two points, (c)
and (d) provide the seed of the separation between the intellect and time, a development from the distinction between inner sense and the faculty of apperception, and the
problem posed by the independent origin of the categories.

There remain, then, two further questions.  What
is there in Kant's system which would suggest Bergson's
claim that time is the ultimate reality?  And what is there
to suggest that intellectual functions should be associated
with space?  We must now attempt to determine what relation,
if any, obtains between Kant and Bergson on these two
points.

## 214

3. <u>Primordial Time and the Spatializing Intellect</u>

The two points we are to deal with here are so
closely connected that we must treat them in relation to
one another. For Bergson's assertion of the metaphysical
primacy of time involves him in the view that there is an
intimate connection between space and the functions of the
intellect. Indeed, the very method he takes in attempting
to answer the question of how inner and outer sense are
related consists in large part in showing how it is that
the intellect breaks up the flow of time into discrete,
spatial parts. In the nature of things, therefore, it is
natural that Bergson's solution to this problem does not
consist in a logical explanation, but consists rather in
showing that a logical explanation of the relation between
space and time is impossible. As we have pointed out in
Chapter Two, Section One, above, a theory which makes a
fundamental distinction between space and time has only a
limited number of possible ways of explaining the relation
between these distinct entities. Bergson, as we have seen,
fully accepts the implications stemming from the point
that the duration which is revealed in inner sense cannot
be adequately represented in concepts. By this token, he
makes it impossible to explain the relation between inner
and outer sense, and hence between space and time, in

rational t:r.c. "is explanation therefore leans heavily
on an appeal to intuition.

The app al to an intuitive grasp of time and space
is not in itself, of course, wholly foreign to Kant's
views, because time and space for him are, above all, pure
intuitions. Then Kant tells us that no man can possibly
answer the question of how in a thinking subject an outer
intuition is possible, 265 however, he reveals his conviction
that philosophy must be li ited to the rational explanation
of the possibility of knowledge. Where reason itself can
make no progress, as in speculations which extend beyond
the sphere of possible experience, reason must desist from
further inquiry. But Bergson does not believe that philosophy must stop there, namely, with the explanation of
the possibility of empirical knowledge. Metaphysics may
proceed by means of intuition,- not indeed the intellectual
intuition which Kant thought would be necessary if there
were to be a knowledge of things-in-themselves, but an intuition which carries us into the heart of the duration
revealed in our own inner consciousness.

> For, in order to reach intuition it is not
> necessary to t .1 .ort ourselves outside the domain
> of the senses and of consciousness. Kant's error
> was to believe that it was. After having proved by
> decisive arguments that no dialectical effort will
> ever introduce us into the beyond and that an effect-
> ive metaphysics would necessarily be an intuitive
> metaphysics, he added that we lack this intuition

and that this metaplysics is im ossiblc.  It would in fact be so if there were no other tine or change than those which Kant perceived and which, moreover, we too must reck.on with; . . .266

Bergson goes on to say that there is another kind of time than that which has been spatialized by the senses and consciousness (which tends to spatialize time in the interests of action).  If we can undo this work of spatialization, we shall have a new kind of knowledge, an intuition of real time.

> Intuition doubtless admits of many de rees of intensity, and philosophy many degrees of depth; but the mind once brought back to real duration will already be alive with intuitive life and its knowledge of things will already be philosophy.  Instead of a discontinuity of moments replacing one another in an infinitely divided time, it will perceive the continuous fluidity of real time which flows along, indivisible.   267

What relation has this view of time as "one identical change which keeps ever lengthening", ·268 to Kant's theory of time as a form of sensibility, and a pure intuition?  Bergson's view seems to be a logical result of Kant's in that Bergson carries out the implications of Kant's admission that there is no substance which persists through changes of state in inner sense.  Kant's theory of time as a form of intuition presupposes that there may be matter (of appearances) which can appear in this form.  But it seems clear that there can be no distinction between matter and form in inner sense.  Since the <u>appearances,</u>

themselves, in inner sense, are not subject to categorical
determination, which provides for the formal features of
appearances, it is difficult to see how, in this area of
appearances matter can be distinguished from form. Kant,
himself, supports this conclusion by saying that in inner
sense no <u>determinate</u> intuition is to be met with. But if
it is not possible to distinguish between time as a form
and the appearances which permeate one another in the flux
of inner sense, we seem to be forced to identify the form
with the flux itself, or rather, to speak more accurately,
to say that time is not a form at all, but is the indivisible change in inner sense itself. Bergson's theory of
time, then, in this respect is a logical development of
that of Kant.

Thus Bergson's intuition of time as duration is
an intuition with a concrete content, but a content which
is not broken up in itself into differentiated parts. Time,
for Bergson, is definitely not an abstract entity. It is
not an abstract becoming, but is  unique, specific change
itself.

> The trick of our perception, like that of our
> intelligence, like that of our language, consists in
> extracting from these profoundly different becomings
> the single representation of becoming <u>in general</u>, un-
> defined becoming, a mere abstraction which by itself
> says nothing and of which, indeed, it is very rarely
> that we think. To this idea, always the same, and
> always obscure or unconscious, we then join, in each

particular case, on  or sever l cl  r images that
re re  t t t      'ich  rv      i tin i ' ll
beco in s ro    t er.  It is t is co osition
of      ifi     fi ite  t t  it  c  e in
ener l  d undefin d t t  e substitu e for the
  cific c  n e.   )

ut  y  ou  er son e u te t i  c crete ti e
wit  ulti te re lit  h t is t ere in K nt t t i 't
su est t is furt r devplo nt   re we to u osc th t
in this c se Ber son's t eo y o s ot re resent a lo ic l
development fro t t of  t  e sh ll try to sho  here
that if this furth r point o es ot re resent the only
lo ical develo it fro  rt, th re  re   ny r te ny
re sons w ic  su est th t at le st ergson's c ntention
represents <u>one</u> c nsistent line of develo ent from Kant.

e hav  alreacy s n th t inn r s se, for K nt,
shares i one res ect, the role of th ngs- -themselves,
in that the a earances     er sense re not subject to
the categories,  nd must be considered aradoxically enou h,
to be, technically s eaking, beyond all possi le experience.
Althou h these ar earances are outside of possible experience in K nt's sense of the ter , they are certainly not
psycholo ically i ossible.  for e are ir ediately aware
of them, and Kant himself ust have held that we were
i mediately a are of the  or he could never have pointed
to the fact of the flux of inner sense as a point hostile
to the rational doctrine of the soul.  If one were to
identify t is etero eneous flux with time itself, as

Bergson does, (since it is not an abstract form), one might be led to a view that in our immediate apprehension of it, we were in contact with its reality itself. If the mark of the ultimately real is something, which *is* in itself quite apart from our ways of knowing things, and we are directly aware of it *as it is*, and not by means of our categorical ways of knowing, not, that is, as a appearance, we must admit that we are *ipso facto* aware of the ultimately real. The flux of inner sense corresponds to these requirements. It is not subject to the categories. We do not know it by means of the categories. Yet we are immediately aware of it. It is not a mere form, because it has an indubitable content. It must, therefore, be something ultimately real. Hence, also, as we have pointed out before, it is misleading to speak of *appearances* of inner sense.

There is a further reason, however, for contending that time is an ultimate reality, and this as well stems from the fact that we are immediately aware of change in inner sense. Kant has seen this objection and attempted to meet it. His statement of it and his reply to it are as follows.

> Against this theory, which admits the
> empirical reality of time, but denies its absolute
> and transcendental reality, I have heard men of
> intelligence so unanimously voicing an objection,

that I must suppose it to occur spontaneously to
every reader to whom this way of thinking is unfa-
miliar.  The objection is this.  Alterations are
real, this being proved by change of our own repre-
sentations-- even if all outer appearances, together
with their alterations, be denied.  Now alterations
are possible only in time, and time is therefore
something real.  There is no difficulty in meeting
this objection. I grant the whole argument.  Certainly
time is something real, namely, the real form of
inner intuition.   270

But Kant's reply does not touch the core of the

difficulty, as Paton points out.

> Kant takes the contention to be that we are
> aware of our ideas (or inner states) as changing in
> time, and he has no difficulty in showing that we are
> equally aware of external objects as in space.  Space
> and time are on precisely the same footing, and if
> one is only the form of appearances, so also is the
> other.  The objector does not, however, mean that he
> is aware of his ideas, or inner states, as in time.
> He means that his awareness is also in time, or is a
> temporal succession.  His contention is that time has
> a very special reality, because it is implied, not
> merely in what he is aware of, but in his awareness
> of it.  What he is aware of may be mere appearance:
> his awareness of it cannot be mere appearance, but
> must be absolute reality.  And if this is so, time
> must be, not merely empirically, but absolutely,
> real.   271

Paton goes on to supply for Kant a more effective

answer to this more stringently phrased objection.  His reply

consists in saying that even if it be granted that time is

implied in our awareness of appearances, we must be aware

of our awareness of these appearances, and if it is supposed

that <u>this</u> awareness, (of awareness) is also in time, we

embark on an infinite regress.  At any stage of this

infinite re ress, Kant can contend that time is merely the
empirically real for  of what we are aware of, and not
implied in awareness itself.  This is a highly ingenious
reply, and must be exa ined with care.

First of all, we note that the thing which Paton,
(and Kant) have to prove is that time is _not_ implied in
awareness, that is, in consciousness itself.  Does Paton's
reply suffice to show this?  We think not.  The bubble of
the objection is immediately deflated when it is pointed
out that even if an indefinitely extended series of aware-
nesses of awareness is involved, this might very well
occur in time.  In fact, it would be a rather strange
thing if our awareness of _anything_ did not take some time.
Thus in speaking of an infinite regress, Paton has merely
dragged in an irrelevancy, and has not shown that time is
not implied in consciousness itself.

It is this point, namely, that we are immediately
aware of duration in our inner experience, and that this
duration is inextricably bound up with our consciousness
that Bergson takes as central to his philosophy.  He tells
us that "The existence of which we are most assured and
which we know best is unquestionably our own", [272] and he
follows Kant in making time a condition of our experience
of this existence.  But unlike Kant, he refuses to separate

from the content of our consciousness, the conscious-

we have of our own existence.  Consciousness becomes

ually synonymous with duration itself.

> The more we succeed in making ourselves con-
> scious of our pro,ress in pure duration, the more we
> feel the different parts of our bein, enter into each
> other, and our whole personality concentrate itself
> in a point, or rather a sharp ed e, pressed against
> the future and cutting into it unceasingly.  It is in
> this that life and action are free.    273

It is to be noted that kant's theory of space and

does not allow one to apply the same kind of argument

rove the absolute reality of space.  For the essential

t in the above argument is that time is <u>always</u> involved

onsciousness.  Space for Kant, however, is not always

lved in consciousness, for time alone is absolutely

ary in the domain of sense.  Space, according to Kant,

he condition of <u>outer</u> appearances only.  As Paton re-

s, "the fact remains that space is said to be the con-
274
on of some human experience, but not of all".   It is

eivable that there might be consciousness without the

ence of space in it, but it is not conceivable, on

's principles, that there should be consciousness

h did not involve time.  It is only because Kant se-

tes the contents of consciousness from the form that

an maintain that time is only empirically real. But

e time is, for Kant, associated with the undeniable

reality of i:ncr consciousness, rather th i the external
world, his view su ests that the reality of consciousness
is necessarily bound up with the reality of time, and
vice versa.  This is Ber_son's doctrine and is, therefore,
a logical development of Iant's.

But this su_gests also that time may be only empirically real and not even transcendentally ideal.  Bergson
accepts this result, but elaborates a new doctrine of
what empiricism should mean.  Traditional empiricism, he
argues, does not start with what is fundamental, but with
what is already derivative and broken up, like a set of
ready-made garments "which will suit Feter as well as Paul
because they do not show off the figure of either".[275]  Bergson's empiricism is different, and is as well the true
metaphysics.

> Mais un empirisme vrai est celui qui se propose
> de serrer d'aussi près que possible l'original lui-
> même, d'en approfondir la vie, et, par une espèce
> d'auscultation spirituelle, d'en sentir palpiter l'ame;
> et cet empirisme vrai est la vraie metaphysique.  [276]

The empirically real in this sense, then, is also
the absolutely real, and time is by the same token the
ultimate reality.  Hence we must conclude that the relation
between the theories of time in Kant and Bergson in this
respect is one of a natural and logical development.

In view of Bergson's acceptance of time as ultimate
reality, wherein does his explanation of the relation between

space and time consist?  It is apparent that the only way
he can explain this relation is by somehow deriving space
from time.  And the only way he can communicate his explanation of how it is that conscious bein s  ve outer intuitions of space is to atter pt to lead us into an intuitive
grasp of this derivation of space from time.  This is, in
fact, the course which Bergson takes.  He invites us first
to make the effort of acquiring an intuition of duration.

> Let us seek, in the depths of our experience,
> the point where we feel ourselves most intimately
> within our own life.  It is into pure duration that
> we then plunge back, a duration in which the past,
> always moving on, is swelling unceasingly with a
> present that is absolutely new.  But, at the same time,
> we feel the spring of our will strained to its ut-
> most.   277

By this means we can have an intuition of reality
itself, and although a complete grasp of it is beyond human powers, we can attain to the intuition of duration in
varying de rees.  If we wish to attain the intuition of
space and matter, however, we must reverse this effort
and proceed in the direction of a relaxation of the creative
tension.

> But suppose we let ourselves go and, instead
> of acting, dream.  At once the self is scattered; our
> past, which till then was gathered together into the
> indivisible impulsion it communicated to us, is broken
> up into a thousand recollections made external to one
> another.  They give up interpenetrating in the degree
> that they become fixed.  Our personality thus descends
> in the direction of space.  It coasts around it con-
> tinually in sensation.   278

## 225

Bergson, in effect, agrees with Kant that the intellect, and hence pure concepts, do influence or have an effect on time, but he points out that this is merely a practical exigency. Bergson's acceptance of concrete change as time brings the whole question of the relation between space and time down from the abstract level of pure concepts influencing the pure form of sensible intuition, to the level of a naturalistic explanation of what is involved in our perception of matter and space. Thus the problem which in Kant's terms remains insoluble becomes explainable in psychological and biological terms. But even here psychology and biology are dealt with in terms involving liberal doses of Bergson's doctrine of intuition, and so it becomes questionable whether he is not doing metaphysics throughout, a metaphysics designed to deal with that question concerning the relation between inner and outer sense, which Kant refused to answer. But because Bergson has taken the step of considering time to be the ultimate reality, his explanation of how inner and outer sense come to be related in one experience, and how change in general is possible, rests on a metaphysical explanation of how matter and intelligence arise out of the basic flow of time.

This explanation, however, carries him far beyond anything involved in Kant's position on space and time. It

must cert inly ue said that this aspect of Bergson's thou ht does not represent a lo ical develop ent from ant's position, or p rhaps, that of anyone else. For Bergson's acceptance of time or concrete process as ultimate reality does not nece s rily involve the view that pure concepts must be derived therefrom. We have hitehead's example to show that a different development is possible. Plotinus, whom Bergson resembles in some respects on the explanation of matter, of course, represents the antithesis of Bergson on this matter, as Ber son himself points out.

> ore generally, the relation that we establish in the present chapter between "extension" and "detension" resembles in some aspects that which Plotinus supposes. . .when he makes extension not indeed an inversion of original Being, but an enfeeblement of its essence, one of the last stages of the procession. . . Yet ancient philosophy did not see what consequences would result from this for mathematics, for Plotinus, like Plato, erected mathematical essences into absolute realities. Above all, it suffered itself to be deceived by the purely superficial analogy of duration with extension. It treated the one as it treated the other, regarding change as a degradation of immutability, the sensible as a fall from the intelligible. Whence. . .a philosophy which fails to recognize the real function and scope of the intellect.   279

Thinking along these lines, Bergson can, with a
280
measure of truth accuse Kant of out-and-out Platonizing. All resemblance and development in this respect, then, must be rejected. Nevertheless, Bergson's conceptions of matter and space do resemble those of Kant in content, so that in examining their views in relation to one another, we can

see the point where Bergson's development breaks off and takes a direction quite opposed to  ant's position.

Bergson begins his investigation of the concept of matter fro  a phenomenalist standpoint.  He asks us to put aside all philosophic preconceptions, all latent metaphysics and look out upon the world of outer sense merely as it is.  What do we find there?  We find _images_, and it is in images that Bergson discovers the answer to the question "What is matter?".  The man unaccustomed to the theories of philosophy, Bergson tells us, would be greatly astonished to be told either that objects were only mental existents, or on the contrary that they were things quite unlike the objects he perceives.  Common sense, then, seems to have grasped a fact of prime importance, namely, the self-existent reality of images as images.  Thus matter is an aggregate of images.  As such, it may be treated as a system obeying its own laws quite apart from perception, or it may be regarded as containing a privileged image, namely, that of the body, which conditions all other images, modifying them in quixotic ways.  The former represents the position of realism, the latter of idealism; in one, the mind is an accident, in the other science and its stable laws of nature is an accident.  "But, for both parties, to
261
perceive means above all to know".

## 228

Perception, for Bergson, is a function of the living organism, dependent thereon for its scope and richness, a contention that few would dispute. For Bergson, however, this fact is the basis of important metaphysical conclusions, one of which he states in the form of a general law: "Perception is master of space in the exact measure in which action is master of time".[282] But what does this mastery involve? It involves the active powers of a certain image, the human body, or an animal body, as a centre of action amid the totality of images which make up the universe. Pure perception, that is, perception which is considered apart from the conditioning of memory which accompanies all actual perception, consists in the action of the body image whereby whatever part of other images which may be detached, is detached as the representation of these other images. Thus the representation which appears in consciousness in perception is not a thing apart from the aggregate of images which constitute matter; it is among them, in the relation of a part to a whole. But the perceptual image is not, therefore, identical with the object, because the body cannot lay hold of all of the object image. It can only master what it can master.

> Perception appears, then, only as a choice. It creates nothing; its office, on the contrary, is to eliminate from the totality of images all those on which I can have no hold, and then, from each of those

wł ich I retain, all that does not concern the needs of the i.a e wł ich I call my body.   283

Thus, perception is not, as realism and idealism take it to be, <u>pure knowlec e</u>, w ich, as such, has a wholly speculative interest.   It is rather the <u>action</u> of living centres of indetermination upon other ima es in the totality of matter.

> In other words let us posit that system of closely-lin ed ima es which we call t e nat rial world, and imagine here and there, <u>centres of real action</u>, re resentod  y living matter: what we mean to  rove is that <u>there  ust</u> be, ran ed round each one of these centres, i a s that are subordinated to its position and variable  with it; that conscious perce tion is bound to occur. . . 284

But o posed to  ure perce tion, that is, radically different from it in kind, is pure memory, a thing of the spirit.   Bergson rejects the Hobbesian theory that memory is weakened or decayed sense.   Nor are me ories stored up in the brain.   ure perception is a mere extreme which, if it were ever actual, would be instantaneous; but our actual perce tion has duration, and the difference is due to memory, the welling-up of the past into the present.

> In concrete perception memory intervenes, and the subjectivity of sensible qualities is due precisely to the fact that our consciousness, which begins by being only memory, prolon s a plurality of moments into each other, contracting them into a single in- tuition.   285

Thus every concrete perception is "a synthesis, made by memory, of an infinity of pure perceptions which

## 230

286

succeed one anot'er".  'Here _ain we h've Bergson's doctrine of the qualitative synthesis, quite unlike that due
to pure concepts and a transcendental unity of apperception.  Perceived objects  re indeed the result of a synthesis, just .s Kant, in a different way, and according
to different principles, thought they were.  It is for
Bergson a synthesis which holds together the results of
a succession of pure perceptions in time.  These pure perceptions are fragments detached from the totality of
images, parts of the totality of images which makes up
the material world, for "images outrun perception on every

287

side".  But the agency which performs this synthesis is
not thought but memory, and the synthesis is a qualitative
one not a quantitative one.  Thus the multiplicity of objects in the natural world of experience is brought about
not by ordering principles which stem from pure concepts
of the understanding, but by the practical exigencies of
life and the agency of memory.  Thus, Bergson, like Kant,
follows the requirements of the theory we have called
possibility B, out unlike Kant the means whereby he explains objects in space is partly psychological and
biological.  Nevertheless, perceived objects in space
are the result of principles or agencies which act through
the medium of time.  The principle or agency in Bergson's
case is, of course, pure memory.  This raises the question

o_ to what extent in Bergson's syste  material objects are distinct fro  one another in nature.

Bergson tells us that "That there are, in a sense, multiple objects, that one man is distinct from another man, tree from tree, stone from stone, is an indisputable fact".[288]  But in reality these objects are not so distinct as they appear in our perception, for "to perceive consists in condensing enormous periods of an infinitely diluted existence into a few more differentiated moments of an intenser life".[289]  To perceive means to immobilize, and all this is done in the interests of life.  Distinct, sharply separated bodies are marked out and distinguished only in the practical interests of life and action.

It is difficult to say to what extent bodies in the external world have an independent existence, for Bergson, if indeed, they have any.  Matter as an aggregate of images is "an existence placed half-way between the 'thing' and the 'representation'".[290]  It is difficult to understand exactly what Bergson means by this spatial metaphor. Perhaps the best way of grasping his meaning is to approach it from the standpoint of distinctness itself.  The 'thing' for Bergson, in its clear-cut distinctness, is an unreality, a fiction of the intellect, employed for purely practical purposes.  The 'representation', as a purely

syc olo ic l e.tit , _ sen tio , . iich i  b olutely
inextensive, is cl e ot r extre e of t' is unsatisfactory
dichotomy.    hat is real is somewhere between the two
in distinctness.

That w icl is iven, that  iic'. is real,
is so ethin  inter ediate between  ivided extension
and pure inextension.  It is what we have turned
ext sive.  Extensit  is t e 10 t salient qu lity
of perception. 291

Space as  n absolute, homo eneous  ediu  emer es
in Bergson's treatme t  s not lo ically prior to material
things, but  os erior to t en, "like an infinitely fine
network which we stretch beneath material continuity in
order to render ourselves  aster of it, to deco pose it
according to the  lan of our activities and needs".
It is a mistake to re ard this homo eneous space a
a thin , as a le itimate object of speculative interest,
when at bottom abstract space is "nothin  but the mental
diagram of infinite divisibility",   which has arisen as
a fiction of the imagination in the interests of the
needs of life.

There is much similarity between Bergson's account
of space and that of Kant, althou , of course, in Kant,
as re ards the genesis of space, we find no equivalent to
Bergson's vitalism.  Bergson, indeed, explicitly agrees
with Kant in re arding space as a for  of sensibility.

> so we have assumed the existence of a
> homogeneous space, and with it, distinguished
> this space from the matter which fills it. With
> him we have admitted that homogeneous space is a
> "form of our sensibility". . . 294

Bergson's professed agreement with Kant, however, is somewhat misleading. For, as his later writings abundantly show, Bergson agrees with Kant only in what Kant denied, namely, a knowledge of the ultimately real by means of concepts. [295] Although Bergson agrees with Kant to the extent that they both, in different ways, follow the theory we have called possibility (B), it is apparent that he rejects the whole Kantian point of view, when he derives the intellect itself from primordial duration. He agrees that Kant's Transcendental Aesthetic "appears to have established once for all that extension is not a material attribute of the same kind as the others". [296] But Bergson's conception of this "form of sensibility" proves to be radically different from Kant's. He reviews the three metaphysical possibilities which Kant had conceived: "either the mind is determined by things, or things are determined by the mind, or between mind and things we must suppose a mysterious agreement", [29] but he also proposes a fourth possibility, which he takes to be the correct one.

his alternative consists, first of all, in
regarding the intellect as a special function of the
mind, essentially turned toward inert matter; then
in saying that neither does matter determine the form
of the intellect, nor does the intellect impose its
form on matter, nor have matter and intellect been
regulated in regard to one another by we know not
what pre-established harmony, but that intellect and
matter have progressively adapted themselves one to
the other in order to attain at last a common form.
This adaptation has, moreover, been brought about
quite naturally, because it is the same inversion of
the same movement which creates at once the intel-
lectuality of mind and the materiality of things. 298

This passage follows after Bergson's explanation

for Kant, "space is given as a ready-made form of our

ptive faculty-- a veritable deus ex machina, of which

e neither how it arises, nor why it is what it is

r than anything else". 299 So we can only conclude that

er or not Bergson would stand by his early agreement,

ant that space is a form of sensibility, his final

ption of space is quite unlike that of Kant.  It is

itely not a priori in Kant's sense.  Whether Bergson's

y of space fulfills the same function as Kant's,

y, of justifying the applicability of geometry to the

al world, is highly questionable.  Bergson believes

his theory does this.

   ....there is this about it (space) that is
remarkable that our mind, speculating on it with its
own powers alone, cuts out in it, a priori, figures
whose properties we determine a priori: experience,
with which we have not kept in touch, yet follows us

ut i    it  of tli  wi c ivergence between these
two thinker , t'.eir theories of the conce t of homo-eneous
space and its rel tion to the s _ce of sensible experience
bear a ar'ed similarity.  The absoluteness and infinitude
of space, for exam le, is in Kant's view a mere idea, the
work of reason.

> To assume an absolute space, that is, one
> which, because it i- not mat_rial, c n be no object
> of ex erience as ~ive.1 for itself, means assuming
> somethin whic! , ieither in itself nor in its con-
> sequences (.:otion in absolute space), can be perceived,
> for tl e sake of the ossibility of experience, which
> neverthelesa ust always exist without it.  Absolute
> s. ce is in itself nothing and no object at all, but
> signifies merely every other relative space that I
> can at any time c        outside the given space, and
> that I can extend beyond each given space to infinity;
> one that includes the given space and in which I can
> assume it as moved.  But since I have the enlarged,
> although still material space only in thought, nothing
> is known to me of the matter indicating it.  I abstract
> from this, and it is conceived, therefore, as a pure,
> non-empirical and absolute space. . . 301

The conception of absolute space is reached then
by reasoning from given empirical spaces.  Absolute space
is the logical limit of the expansion of finite spaces.
It is just in this fashion, Bergson argues, that Newton,
Euler and others arrived at the notion of absolute space.

> A place could be absolutely distinguis'.ed
> from another place only by its quality or by its
> relation to the totality of space: so that space
> would become, on this hypothesis, either composed
> of heterogeneous parts or finite.  But to finite
> space we should ive another space as boundary,
> and beneath heterogeneous parts of space we should
> imagine an homogeneous space as its foundation: in
> both cases it is to homogeneous and indefinite space
> that we should necessarily return. 302

Similarly, as might be expected, the divisibility

ogeneous space is another feature common to the

nes of both Kant and Bergson. And for both, this

bility is a function of the intellect.

> The whole of matter is made to appear to our
> hought as an immense piece of cloth in which we can
> ut out what we will and sew it together again as we
> lease. Let us note, in passing, that it is this
> ower that we affirm when we say that there is a
> *pace*, that is to say, a homogeneous and empty medium,
> nfinite and infinitely divisible, lending itself in-
> ifferently to any mode of decomposition whatsoever.
> medium of this kind is never perceived; it is only
> onceived. 303

Kant tells us that "the space that is filled by

is mathematically divisible to infinity",[304] and

r, that "mathematics can indeed. . .rest in the

n possession of its evident assertions of the in-

divisibility of space".[305] At the same time, Kant is

as to point out that this infinite divisibility of

is not a property of space as thing-in-itself, but

ely due to the possibility of conceiving in thought

finite divisibility of a given space.

> Thus we can only say of phenomena, the divisior
> f which goes on to infinity, that there exist so many
> f the parts of the phenomenon, as we give of them,
> hat is, as far as we can ever subdivide. *For the*
> *arts, as belonging to the existence of a phenomenon*
> *xist only in thought, namely, in their division*
> *tself.* 306

Matter, for Kant, although not described in terms

ges, is similar to Bergson's view of matter in that

it is sensed, or felt,— ct r is material. It is defined as the "movable in space", and its sensible character is revealed in Kant's remark in which he makes the
distinction between matter and form.

>... matter, in contradistinction to _form_, would
be that which in external intuition, is an object of
feeling, and consequently the properly empirical of
sensible and outward intuition, because it cannot be
given at all _a priori_. In all experience something
must be felt, and this is the real of sensuous intuition.   308

Thus, for both Kant and Bergson the divisibility
of space in the matter, as sensed, which fills it, is
not a property of what is actually sensed, but is introduced by means of the intellect through the mathematical
conception of the infinite divisibility of space as an
object of thought. Their reasons for holding this in
one case, however, are different. For Kant the reason
consists in the point that space as an object of thought
is different, in some manner which Kant does not fully
explain, from the pure intuition of space, _pure_ intuition.
His view seems to be that a given empirical space is
_potentially_ divisible, and this is due, no doubt, to the
fact that as a continuous quantity it has been synthesized.
The pure intuition of space in so far as it is divisible
provides the basis of division which in itself is a mathematical construction. Hence although a given space is
potentially divisible, we cannot say it has an infinite

num er o° parts, bec'us  it 's thus divisiblo only so far
as 'e divide it.

On the oth r hand Ber son maintains, as we have
seen, t'' t  atter is somewhere between pure inextension
and infi.ite extension.  As such it is extensive but has
not ¿ot .ll the properties whicn pertain to homogeneous
space.  'atter arises from the aegradation of the extra-
spatial into spatiality, but the process does not go on to
absolute co.pletior.  The intellectual idea of pure space
"is only the schema of the limit at which this movement
would end".  309  Spatiality admits of degrees, and "matter
extends itself in space without being absolutely extended
therein".  310  Thus, in Bergson's view, there are two kinds
of space, or rather different degrees of spatiality,- the
one exemplified in matter, a kind not carried to complete
spatiality,- the other a thing of the intellect, infinite,
indefinitely divisible, homogeneous.  This exhibits the
main difference between kant's view of the relation of the
intellect to space, and that of Bergson.  There is no evidence to su_gest that kant thought that spatiality could
admit of degrees.  The sharp distinction between inner and
outer sense, in any ca se, would preclu e this.  Nevertheless, the two kinds of spatiality in Bergson's philosophy
are related in exactly the same way as are kant's relative,
empirical space, which is felt or sensed, and the absolute

space which is ... logical limit of the conceptual expansion of finite spaces. In each case, the absolute space is regarded as the limit towards which the other tends. But the character of the tendency is different. With Bergson, the tendency from inextension to absolute spatiality, and also the notion of so et in which lies between these limits, is highly obscure. In the absence of the requisite intuition, one can only fall back on the logical conception of continuity, which, indeed, Bergson himself exploits in attempting to co ...ac·te this doctrine. May we conclude that Bergson is perhaps unwittingly introducing the concept of space here, and that his doctrine represents the ghost of Kant's logical expansion of spaces? In this case, we might be entitled to conclude that Bergson's doctrine of space, and even its derivation from the non-spatial is not so very different from Kant's. But here, unfortunately, we are faced with a point which can never be decided by rational argument.

Bergson thinks that the intellect is characterized by a latent geometry, which makes it operate the way it does. He goes so far in this direction as to suggest that deduction itself is due to this latent geometry, which "is immanent in our idea of space",[311] and that from this latent geometry arises logic. In the face of this interpretation of logic, all comparison between Kant and Bergson

must come to a halt. Bergson is gracious enough to
see that from the point of view of the intellect, there
is a <u>petitio principii</u> in making geometry arise automatically from space, and logic from geometry".[312]   It is, of
course, just because Bergson does not share the point of
view of the intellect that he differs so radically from
Kant. Thus, Bergson's development of some aspects of
Kant's thought ends in a view which, for Kant, would probably represent "the chicanery of a falsely instructed
reason .

tried Martin, Kant's Metaphysics and Theory of Science,
s. P.G. Lucas (Manchester: The Manchester University
s, 1955), p. 11.


anuel Kant, Critique of Pure Reason, trans. Norman Kemp
h (London: Macmillan & Co., Ltd., 1955), p. 68. Sub-
ent references to this work will be designated "Critique",
both the page number of the translation and that of
first and second editions of the original work will be
.


w. Meinecke, "Die Bedeutung der nichteuklidischen
atrie", Kantstudien XI, 1906. H.J. Paton, Kant's
physics of Experience, (London: George Allen & Unwin,
). Gottfried Martin, Kant's Metaphysics and Theory of
ace.


ald C. Williams, "The Myth of Passage", Journal of Philo-
y, XLVIII, no. 15, July (1951), p. 457.


D. Lindsay, The Philosophy of Bergson, (London: J...
& Sons, 1911), pp. 2-3.


predo Kant historical influence on Bergson seems to
been French, although the direct and indirect influence
erman philosophy cannot be ignored. In this regard
Ben-Ami Scharfstein, Roots of Bergson's Philosophy,
York: Columbia University Press, 1943).


haps the most notable difference between the measure-
of space and the measurement of time, is that spatial
ths can sometimes be compared, side by side, in sen-
s intuition, while it is impossible to take one "chunk"

Ernst Cassirer, Substance and Function and Einstein's Theory of Relativity, trans. William Curtis Swabey and Marie Collins Swabey (Chicago-London: The Open Court Publishing Company, 1923), p. 105. (Italics not in text).

9

John Alexander Gunn, The Problem of Time, (London: George Allen & Unwin, 1929), p. 371.

10

Ibid., pp. 373-374.

11

Cf. Samuel Alexander, Space, Time and Deity, London, 1934.

12

H. Minkowski, "Space and Time", in H.A. Lorentz, A. Einstein, H. Minkowski, and H. Weyl, The Principle of Relativity, trans. W. Perrett and G.B. Jeffery, with notes by A. Sommerfield (London: Methuen & Co., 1923), p. 75.

13

George Gamow, One, Two, Three. . .Infinity, (New York: The Viking Press, 1947), p. 88.

14

This is a view which Kant, himself, combats. Cf, Critique, pp. 80-81, A39, B56. ("A" refers to the page number of the first edition, "B" to that of the second).

15

Ethics, I, Def. 3.

16

Ethics, I, Prop. 3.

17

Cf. The Problems of Philosophy, (London: Williams & Norgate, Ltd., 1912); also Mysticism and Logic (London: Longmans, Green & Co., 1918); also Proceedings of the Aristotelian Society, (1910-11).

18

John Locke, An Essay concerning Human Understanding, ed. A. S. Pringle-Pattison (Oxford: Oxford University Press, 1924), Bk. II, Ch. 15, Sec. 12, p. 121.

Alfred North Whitehead, Science and the Modern World,
ambridge: Cambridge University Press, 1926), Cheap Edi-
on  p. 63.


Ibid., p. 62.


bid., p. 62.


bid., p. 70.


Alfred North Whitehead, Adventures of Ideas, (Cambridge:
mbridge University Press, 1933), p. 197.


Alfred North Whitehead, Science and the Modern World, p.158.


Ibid., p. 156.


A.A. Robb, The Geometry of Time and Space, (Cambridge:
mbridge University Press, 1936), p. 19.


Ibid., p. 23.


C.D. Broad, Scientific Thought, (London: Kegan Paul, Trench,
ubner & Co., 1923), p. 217.


Ibid., p. 55.


John Locke, op. cit., Bk. II, Ch. 15, Sec. 1, p. 115.


Ibid., II, 15, Sec, 9, p. 118. It should be noted that
r Locke "time" is a term used for measured duration. The
tter is the basic idea, and the former is derived there-
om by measurement. Locke calls space "expansion" to
stinguish it from extension, "which by some is used to

atter". But Locke is not entirely consistent in this
sage, since, in the same chapter, (II, 15), in which he
akes this distinction, he reverts to using "extension"
s synonymous with space. Cf. Sec. 9.

2
 Ibid., II, 15, Sec. 5, p. 117.

3
 C.D. Broad, Scientific Thought, p. 53.

4
 C.D. Broad, An Examination of McTaggart's Philosophy,
Cambridge: Cambridge University Press, 1933), II, 269.

5
 A.A. Robb, op. cit., pp. 6-7

6
 Ibid., p. 20.

7
 Richard Taylor, "Spatial and Temporal Analogies and the
oncept of Identity", The Journal of Philosophy, LII, No.
2, Oct. (1955), p. 599.

8
 Ibid., p. 600.

9
 Bertrand Russell, Our Knowledge of the External World,
Chicago: The Open Court Publishing Co., 1929), p. 254.

0
 C.D. Broad, Scientific Thought, p. 58.

1
 Ibid., p. 61.

2
 Taylor, op. cit., p. 601.

3
 Ibid., p. 601.

4
 Ibid., p. 602.

Broad, _Scientific Thought_, p. 57.

Taylor, _op. cit._, pp. 610-612.

on Goodman, _The Structure of Appearance_, (Cambridge:
d University Press, 1951), p. 301.

., pp. 300-301.

Broad, _Scientific Thought_, p. 57.

., p. 59.

ld C. Williams, "The Sea Fight Tomorrow", in Henle,
ure, _Method and Meaning_, Essays in Honor of Henry L.
r, (New York: The Liberal Arts Press, 1951), p. 304.

man, _op. cit._, p. 302.

King, "Aristotle and the Paradoxes of Zeno", in _The
l of Philosophy_, XLVI (1949), p. 662.

., p. 667.

rand Russell, _Mysticism and Logic_, (London and New
Longmans Green & Co., 1918), p. 84.

is the view taken by Goodman, who remarks, "Strange]
it turns out not that time is more fluid than (say)
but rather that time is more static". _Op. cit._, p. 3(

Hobbes, Leviathan, Pt. I, Ch. I; also _De Corpore_.

tique, p. 190; A151, B191.

anuel Kant, De Mundi Sensibilis atque Intelligibilis
 et Principiis, trans. John Handyside in Kant's
ural Dissertation and Early Writings on Space, (Chi-
and London: The Open Court Publishing Co., 1929), p.

d., p. 45.

d., p. 65

d., pp. 80-81.

d., p. 65.

tique, pp. 190-191; A152, B191.

dyside, p. 7.

tique, p. 181; A138-9, B177-8.

dyside, p. 56.

d., p. 60.

d.

d., p. 61.

d., p. 58.

tique, p. 67; A22, B36.

itique, p. 204; A169, B211.

id., p. 3?8; A411, B438.

id.

id., p. 388; A412, B439.

id.

id.

id., p. 387; A410, B437.

J. Paton, Kant's Metaphysics of Experience,
(e Allen & Unwin, 1936), I, 123.

itique, p. 581; A720, B748.

ndyside, pp. 64-65.

id., pp. 64-65.

itique, p. 87; A49, B66.

id., p. 349; A374.

id., pp. 67-68; A23, B37.

id., p. 77; A34, B50.

id., p. 232; A210, B255.

89
  Ibid., p. 192; A155, B194.

90
  Ibid., p. 166; B154.

91
  Ibid., p. 136; A107.

92
  Ibid., p. 68; A23, B37

93
  Ibid., p. 77; A33, B49.

94
  Ibid., p. 56; B20.

95
  Ibid., p. 131; A98-99.

96
  Ibid., p. 133; A101.

97
  Ibid., p. 356; A386-387.

98
  Ibid., p. 348; A372-373.

99
  Ibid., p. 355; A385.

100
  Ibid., p. 68; A23, B37.

101
  G. F. Stout, A Manual of Psychology,  th Ed. p. 496.

102
  Critique, p. 255; B291.

103
  Ibid., p. 136; A107.

104
  Ibid., p. 87; B67.

Stout, _op. cit._, p. 496.

F. C. Bartlett, "Problems in the Psychology of Temporal
Perception", in _Philosophy_, XII (1937), p. 461.

Ibid., p. 463.

Kant's theory of space and time, however, has been
profoundly misunderstood by some psychologists. For example,
my Sturt's comment on a passage from the _Transcendental
Aesthetic_:  "Time cannot be a priori in the Kantian sense,
because knowledge of it both develops in the individual
and appears to vary in different cases", is, of course,
irrelevant.  (M. Sturt, _The Psychology of Time_, p. 10.

_Critique_, p. 87; A49, B66.

Ibid., pp. 72, 80; A28, B44; A39, B56.

Ibid., p. 87; B66.

Ibid., p. 77; A34, B51.

Ibid., pp. 346-347; A371.

Ibid., p. 351; A378.

Ibid., p. 351; A378.

Ibid., p. 348; A373.

Ibid., pp. 239-240; A220, B267.

Ibid., p. 166; B154.

Critique, p. 165; B152. "In so far as imagination is
spontaneity; I sometimes also entitle it the productive
imagination, to distinguish it from the reproductive imagination, which as such is entirely subject to empirical
laws, the laws, namely, of association. . . .The reproductive
synthesis falls within the domain not of transcendental
philosophy, but of psychology". Empirical laws, of course,
presuppose the transcendental unity of apperception, the
transcendental act of imagination, and the categories.
. the analogy concerning the presuppositions of the reproductive synthesis is not entirely exact, as psychology,
. Kant, is not a science. See below p. 161 et seq.


Critique., p. 167; B1...


"Taken together, the analogies thus declare that all
appearances lie, and must lie, in one nature". Critique,
237; A216, B263.


Critique., p. 209; A177, B220.


Ibid., p. 133; A101.


Ibid., p. 226; A200, B245.


Ibid., p. 77; A34; B51.


Ibid., p. 348; A373.


Ibid., p. 440; A491, B520.


Ibid., p. 256; B293-294.


Ibid., p. 339; A357.


Ibid., p. 341; A362.

d., p. 352; A379.

d., p. 77; 33, 49-50.

d., p. 192; A155, B194.

d., p. 330; A343, B401.

on, _op. cit._, I, 64.

d., I, 65.

_tique_, p. 369; B407.

d., p. 22; B xvii.

d., p. 170; B159-160.

ld Hume, _A Treatise of Human Nature_; ed. Selby-Bigge
d: The Clarendon Press, 1896), Bk I, Pt. 3, Sec. XII,
.

on, _op. cit._, I, 556.

_tique_, p. 185; A145, B184.

d., p. 212; A181, B223-224.

d., p. 238; A217, B264.

d., p. 237; A215, B262.

146
 Critique, p. ~??; 210, B255. German text: Immanuel Kant, Sämtliche Werke, ed. J. H. von Kirchmann, (Heidelberg: Georg Weiss, 1891), I, 223. Italics in English version not in text.

147
  tique, p. 232; 210-211, B256.

148
 Ibid., p. 261; A241, B300.

149
 Ibid., p. 251; A233, B286.

150
 Ibid., p. 236; A215, B262.

151
 Ibid., p. 196; .160, B199.

152
 Ibid., p. 184; A143, B182.

153
 Ibid., pp. 166-167; B154.

154
 Ibid., p. 167; B154.

155
 Ibid., p. 112; A78, B104.

156
 Ibid., p. 204; A170, B211-212.

157
 Ibid., p. 295; A291, B347.

158
 Ibid., p. 68; A24, B38-39.

159
 Ibid., p. 198; A163, B203.

160
 Ibid., p. 199; A163, B204.

Ibid., p. 167; A154.

162
    Ibid., p. 167; B154-155. (Kant's footnote).

163
    Ibid., p. 167; B154-155. (First italics not in text).

164
    Ibid., p. 167; B155.

165
    Ibid., p. 182; A139-140, B169-170.

166
    Ibid., p. 183; A142, B181.

167
    Paton, op. cit., II, 78.

168
    Critique, p. 376; B420.

169
    This is a paradox because the metaphysical theory of
the manifold is supposed to account for all contents of
the universe without residue.  In what does the individuality of the consciousness, which is limited to certain
finite regions at certain times, and yet continues the
same in different regions at other times, consist?

170
    Critique, p. 136, A107.

171
    Henri Bergson, Creative Evolution, trans. Arthur Mitchell
(New York: The Modern Library, Random House, Inc., 1944),
p. 3.

172
    Critique, p. 291; A285, B341.

173
    Ibid., p. 290; A283, B339.

174
    Ibid., p. 285; A274, B330.

id., p. 166; A153.

...rson, Creative Evolution, pp. 5-6.

...tique, p. 352; B371.

id., p. 209; A177, B219.

id., p. 204; A170, B211.

id., p. 67; A23, B37.

id., p. 75; A31, B47.

id., p. 348; A373.

id., p. 282; A270, B326.

...manuel Kant, Metaphysical Foundations of Natural
...ce trans. Ernest Belfort Bax in Kant's Prolegomena
...etaphysical Foundations of Natural Science, (London
... Bell and Sons, 1891), p. 140. References to this
...will be hereinafter designated "Bax".

...x, p. 137.

id., p. 222.

...ltique, p. 332, A347, B405.

id., pp. 352-353; A381.

id., p. 255; B291.

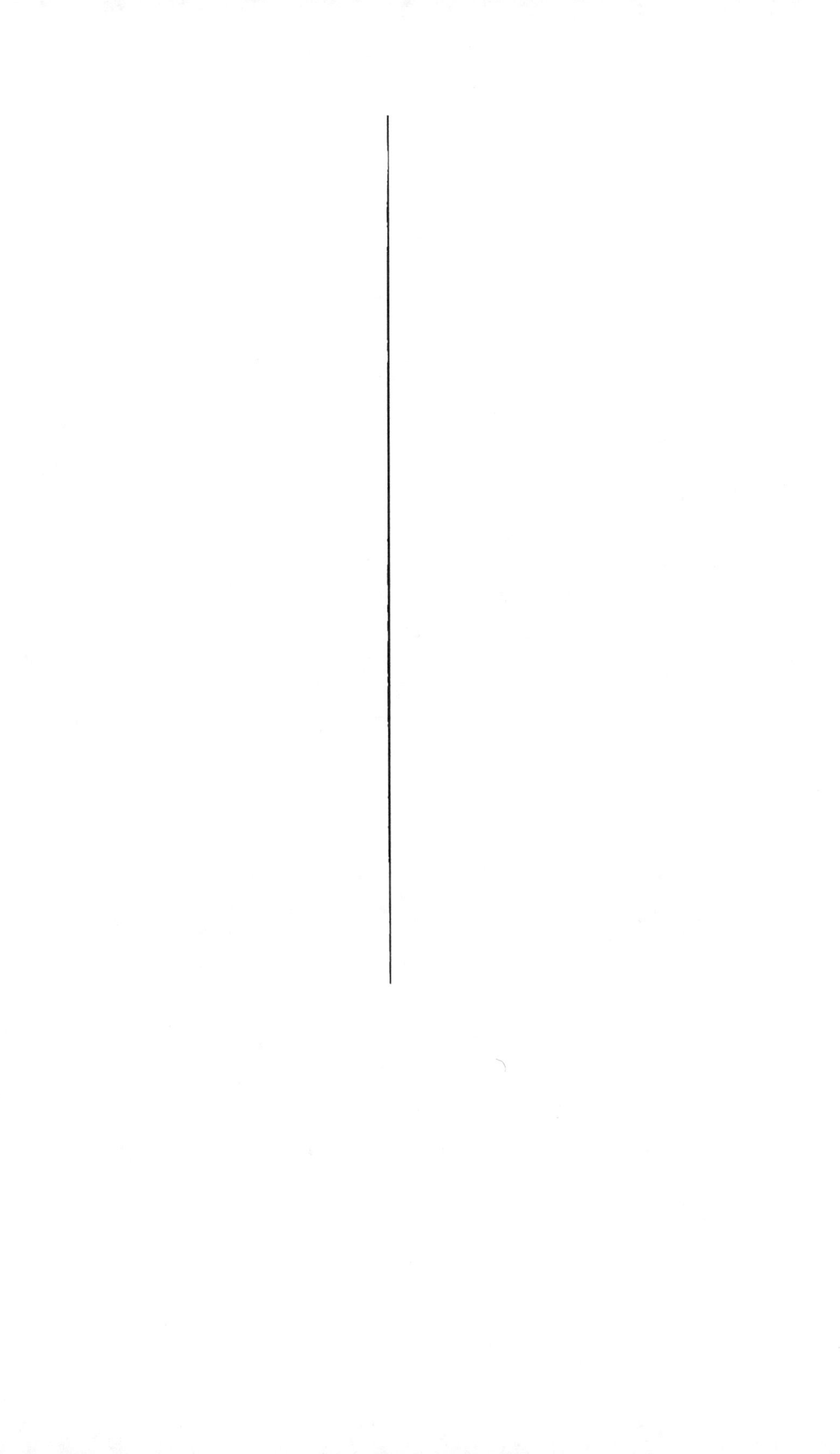

Id., p. 344; A304.

Id., p. 353; A354.

Id., p. 214; A183, B226.

Id.,

Id., p. 255; B292

Id., p. 254; B291.

Id., p. 353; A381.

x, p. 221.

itique, p. 373; B415.

x, pp. 140-141.

id., p. 141.

id.,

y nature, in the empirical sense, we understand the
ction of appearances as regards their existence
ding to necessary rules, that is, according to laws.
are certain laws which first make a nature possible,
hese laws are a priori". Critique, p. 237; A216, B263.


itique, p. 167; B154. (Kant repeats this point
al times throughout the Critique).

ibid., . 141.

ibid.

ibid.

...ri Bergson, "Introduction to Metaphysics", trans.
...lle L. Andison in The Creative Mind (New York: The
...osophical Library, 1946), pp. 191-192.

...bid., p. 191.

...ritique, p. 359; A392-393.

...bid., p. 355; A386-387.

...enri Bergson, Time and Free Will (Essai sur les données
...Immédiates de la conscience) trans. F.L. Pogson (London:
...ge Allen & Unwin, 1910), p. 100.

...ax, p. 141

...enri Bergson, "The Perception of Change", trans. Mabelle
...Andison, in The Creative Mind, p. 173.

...ergson, Time and Free Will, p. 122.

...bid., p. 106.

...ritique, p. 17; B viii.

...G.F. Hegel, The Science of Logic, trans. W.H. Johnston
...L.G. Struthers, 2nd Ed., (London: George Allen & Unwin,
...), I, 39.

time, p. 77; A33, B49-50.

d., p. 204; A169, B211.

d., p. 196; A162, B203. (Kant's German "Nun ist das
...des ...multiplikation Gleichartigen in der
...überhaupt. . ." would seem to be less awkwardl
...ed as ". . . consciousness of the homogeneous mani-
...tuition in general. . ."

d., p. 581; A720, B748.

d., p. 153; A102. Italics not in text.

...son, Time and Free Will, p. 75.

d., p. 77.

d., p. 76.

...anuel Kant, Prolegomena to any Future Metaphysics,
...Paul Carus, Reprint ed. (Chicago and London: The
...ourt Publishing Co., 1949), Sec. 11, p. 36.

tique, p. 198; A162, B203.

d., p. 199; A163, B204.

d., p. 255; B292.

d., p. 255; B291.

d., p. 255; B292.

on, op. cit., II, 279-280.

el..., .. A14; A183, B226.

..., p. 3 ; A412, B439.

..., p. 356; A412, B439.

..., p. 214, A163; B225.

gson, Time and Free Will, p. 67.

tique, p. 112; A76, B104.

...

gson, Time and Free Will, p. 80.

..., p. 61.

..., pp. 62-63.

tique, p. 199-200; A164, B205.

..., p. 168; B156.

gson, Time and Free Will, p. 232.

..., p. 234.

on, op. cit., I, 129.

..., I, 128.

Ibid.

Critique, p. 217; A108, B232.

Ibid., pp. 241-242; A362.

Bergson, Time and Free Will, p. 90.

Henri Bergson, Durée et Simultanéité, 2nd ed. enlarged, (Paris: Librairie Felix Alcan, 1923), Ch. 3, p. 54.

Ibid., p. 55.

Bergson, "The Perception of Change", in The Creative Mind, p. 176.

This, in itself, has its difficulties, as for example Hegel's transition from the Absolute Idea to Nature.

Critique, p. 146; A124.

Ibid., p. 162; A140, B179.

Bergson, Time and Free Will, p. 110.

Ibid., p. 111.

Bergson, "Introduction to Metaphysics" in The Creative Mind, p. 195

Norman Kemp Smith, A Commentary to Kant's Critique of Pure Reason, 2nd Ed. rev. & enl., (London: Macmillan, 1930),

Bergson, "Introduction to Metaphysics" in The Creative
Mind, p. 190.

Henri Bergson, "Life and Consciousness" in Mind-Energy,
tr. H. Wildon Carr (London: Macmillan, 1920), p. 13.

Critique, p. 359; 393.

Bergson, "Philosophical Intuition" in The Creative
Mind, p. 151.

Ibid., p. 150.

Ibid.

Bergson, Creative Evolution, pp. 330-331.

Critique, p. 79; A36-37, B53.

Paton, op. cit., I, 182.

Bergson, Creative Evolution, p. 3.

Ibid., p. 220.

Paton, op. cit., I, 146.

Bergson, "Introduction to Metaphysics", in The Creative
Mind, pp. 206-207.

Ibid., p. 206. French text:- "Introduction a la Méta-
physique" in La Pensée et Le Mouvant, Oeuvres Complètes
Henri Bergson, (Geneva: Editions Albert Skira, 1946),
188.

Bergson, Creative Evolution, p. 21 -219.

Ibid., pp. 220-221.

Ibid., p. 230.

Bergson, "Introduction to Metaphysics", in Creative
d, pp. 232-233.

Henri Bergson, Matter and Memory, trans. Nancy Margar
l and W. Scott Palmer (London: George Allen & Unwin,
1), p. 17.

Ibid., p. 23.

Ibid., p. 304.

Ibid., p. 21.

Ibid., p. 292.

Ibid., p. 238.

Ibid., p. 305.

Ibid., pp. 277-278.

Ibid., p. 275.

Ibid., p. XII.

Ibid., p. 326.

292
   Ibid., p. [illegible].

293
   Ibid., p. 213.

294
   Co., [illegible] Tree Ill, p. 236.

295
   "That is what Kant brought out so clearly and that, it
seems to me, is the greatest service he rendered to speculative philosophy. He definitively established that,
if metaphysics is possible, it can be so only through an
effort of intuition". "The Perception of Change" in The
Creative Mind, p. 165. Thus Bergson agrees with Kant's
denial of the ability of Reason to know ultimate reality.
But, of course, Bergson does not agree with Kant's denial
of a metaphysical intuition.

296
   Bergson, Creative Evolution, p. 223.

297
   Ibid., p. 225.

298
   Ibid., pp. 225-226.

299
   Ibid., p. 224.

300
   Ibid., p. 223.

301
   Bax, p. 151.

302
   Bergson, Matter and Memory, p. 256.

303
   Bergson, Creative Evolution, p. 172.

304
   Bax, pp. 176-177.

305
   Ibid., p. 179.

306
   Ibid., pp. 180-181. Italics not in text.

307
   Ibid., p. 150.

308
   Ibid., p. 151.

309
   Bergson, Creative Evolution, p. 221.

310
   Ibid., p. 223.

311
   Ibid., p. 230.

312
   Ioid., p. 232.

. Only ...s referred to in the text are listed.


... SOURCES


son, Henri . Oeuvres Complètes. Genève: Editions
Albert Skira, 1946.

————. Durée et Simultanéité. Paris: Librairie Felix
Alcan, 1923.

————. Time and Free Will. trans. F. L. Pogson, London:
George Allen & Unwin, 1910.

————. Creative Evolution. trans. Arthur Mitchell,
New York: The Modern Library, Random House, 1944.

————. Matter and Memory. trans. Nancy Margaret Paul
and W. Scott Palmer, London: George Allen & Unwin,
1911.

————. Mind-Energy. trans. H. Wildon Carr, London:
Macmillan, 1920.

————. The Creative Mind. trans. Mabelle L. Andison,
New York: The Philosophical Library, 1946.

————. An Introduction to Metaphysics. trans. T. E.
Hulme; intro. Thomas A. Goudge, New York: The Liberal
Arts Press. 1949.

t, Immanuel . Sämtliche Werke. Ed. J. H. von Kirchmann,
Heidelberg: Georg Weiss, 1891.

————. Kritik der reinen Vernunft. (Vol. I of Works as
above).

————. Kleinere Schriften zur Naturphilosophie. Ed. J.
H. von Kirchmann, Berlin: L. Heimann, 1872.

————. Critique of Pure Reason. trans. Norman Kemp
Smith, London: Macmillan & Co., 1953.

. Metaphysical Foundations of Natural Science. trans. Ernest Belfort Bax, London: George Bell & Sons, 1891.

-----. Prolegomena to any Future Metaphysics. Ed.& trans. Paul Carus, Chicago and London: Open Court Publishing Co., 1949.

-----. Kant's Inaugural Dissertation and Early Writings on Space. trans. John Handyside, Chicago and London: Open Court Publishing Co., 1929.


ARY SOURCES

ks

xander, Samuel. Space, Time and Deity. London, 1934.

ad, C. D. . Scientific Thought. London: Kegan Paul, Trench, Trubner & Co., 1923.

-----. An Examination of McTaggart's Philosophy. Cambridge: Cambridge University Press, 1933.

sirer, Ernst. Substance and Function and Einstein's Theory of Relativity. trans. William Curtis Swabey and Marie Collins Swabey, Chicago and London: Open Court Publishing Co., 1923.

stein, Albert, H. Minkowski, H.A. Lorentz, and H. Weyl. The Principle of Relativity, trans. W. Perrett and G. B. Jeffery, with notes by A. Sommerfield, London: Methuen & Co., 1923.

ow, George. One, Two, Three...Infinity. New York: The Viking Press, 1947.

dman, Nelson. The Structure of Appearance. Cambridge: Harvard University Press, 1951.

n, John Alexander. The Problem of Time. London: George Allen & Unwin, 1929.

el, G.W.F. . The Science of Logic. trans. W.H. Johnston and L.G. Struthers, 2nd Ed., London: George Allen & Unwin, 1951.

Henle, (ed.). Structure, Method and Meaning. New York:
     The Liberal Arts Press, 1951.

Hobbes, Thomas, Leviathan.

————. De Corpore.

Hume, David. A Treatise of Human Nature. ed. Selby-Bigge,
     Oxford: The Clarendon Press, 1896.

Lindsay, A.D.. The Philosophy of Bergson. London: J.M.
     Dent & Sons, 1911.

Locke, John. An Essay concerning Human Understanding. ed.
     A.S. Pringle-Pattison, Oxford: Oxford University
     Press, 1924.

Martin, Gottfried. Kant's Metaphysics and Theory of Science.
     Manchester: Manchester University Press, 1955.

Paton, H.J.. Kant's Metaphysics of Experience. London:
     George Allen & Unwin, 1936.

Robb, A.A.. The Geometry of Time and Space. Cambridge:
     Cambridge University Press, 1936.

Russell, Bertrand. The Problems of Philosophy. London:
     Williams & Norgate, 1912.

————. Mysticism and Logic. London: Longmans, Green &
     Co., 1917.

————. Our Knowledge of the External World. Chicago and
     London: Open Court Publishing Co., 1929.

Scharfstein, Ben-Ami. Roots of Bergson's Philosophy. New
     York: Columbia University Press, 1943.

Smith, Norman Kemp. A Commentary to Kant's Critique of
     Pure Reason. 2nd ed. rev. & enl. London: Macmillan
     & Co., 1930.

Spinoza, Ethics.

Stout, G.F.. A Manual of Psychology. 6th Ed., London:
     Tutorial Press, 1938.

stur, r . _______ ______ __ _ __. _ on: _ega_
  _a_l, 1__5.

_hi___, 1_____ . _ci__c_ _nd ____ _rn _orl_.
  _a___ : __ _ri_ _ _iv_rsi_y _re_s, 192_.

----------. '_ __ __o_l_ ___. _ _ri_ : _ _ri_ _ _ni-
  v_r__y _ress, 1_33.


<u>_r_icles</u>

  rtlett, F.C. . "_roblems in the _sychology of Temporal
     _rce_tic_, _hilosophy, XII (1937).

  _i__, F.__ . "_ristotle and the _aradoxes of _eno", The
     Jo_r__1 o_ P_iloso__y, XLVI (1949).

  _einecke, _. . "Die _deutung _er nichteuklidischen Geo-
     etric", _nt_t_'ien XI, (1906).

  _illia_s, _onald C. . "T_e _yth of _assage" Journal of
     _hil__ op__, XLVIII (1951).

  __ylor, _ichard . "_patial and _emporal An_logies _nd the
     Co_c_ t of I_ _tity", Journal of P_ilosophy, LII
     (1955).

9 780353 293427